THE
CONCERT BAND

THE CONCERT BAND

by

RICHARD FRANKO GOLDMAN

Volume I of the series

THE FIELD OF MUSIC

edited by Ernest Hutcheson, *President Emeritus of the Juilliard School of Music*

RINEHART & COMPANY, INC.

New York · Toronto

PRINTED IN THE UNITED STATES OF AMERICA
BY THE FERRIS PRINTING COMPANY, NEW YORK

Table of Contents

List of Illustrations

Acknowledgments

IN PREPARING this book the author received invaluable help from a number of persons in whose debt he remains. In particular he wishes to thank Alexandra Rienzi, Roger Smith and Mrs. Richard Franko Goldman for many critical readings of the manuscript and for countless helpful suggestions and verifications of fact. Grateful acknowledgment is made to Professor William D. Revelli, Captain George S. Howard, Lieutenant Charles Brendler and Captain James C. Harper, who most kindly provided photographs and first-hand information about their bands; to Lieutenant Colonel Howard C. Bronson for information on U. S. Army bands; and to Dr. Charles O'Neill and Mr. Erik W. G. Leidzen for helpful conversations about bands in general. To Dr. Edwin Franko Goldman the author is indebted not only for most of what he has learned about the band, but also for the use of an immense library of band music and works dealing with bands, and for several rare photographs and prints used in this volume. For permission to reproduce pages of band scores, the author wishes to thank the Leeds Music Corporation, Mercury Music Corporation, and Music Press, Inc., and their representatives.

RICHARD FRANKO GOLDMAN

New York, April 1946

THE CONCERT BAND

CHAPTER I

Introduction: *An Attempt to Define the Nature and Place of the Concert Band*

The term "concert band" is a relatively new one in the musical vocabulary, and one which is not easy to define precisely. Musical terms acquire new definitions from time to time; the vulgarization of musical speech and thought via "popularizing" mediums in the last few decades has contributed still further to the confusion. Thus, "classical music" is in the mass mind almost anything not played for dancing, a "symphony orchestra" is any body of musicians conducted by someone with a publicity staff and long hair, or no hair at all, and a "band" is generally assumed to be a dance orchestra. The "concert band" should be a body of wind instrument players primarily occupied in giving concerts; that is, in performing music of a self-sufficient sort at functions devoted entirely to music. Since wind bands have always been more or less utilitarian in character, the concept of a "concert band" is itself new in comparison to that of the "symphony" or concert orchestra. It is not a long time since such groups of wind players were universally called "military bands"; indeed many of the musical dictionaries appearing in the past few years still refer the reader to the heading "Military Band" for any information about wind bands. The military band was of course the prototype of the present concert band, and many band usages still prevalent, notably the uniforming of the musicians, stem directly from the days when all bands of importance were attached to the military. But the term "military band" is too restrictive to describe either the concert-giving civilian band of professional musicians or the bands which have been so highly developed along functionally different lines in schools, colleges and conservatories.

Military bands still exist, and although they no longer play as troops go into battle (though the awesome idea of a tank-borne band has been seriously advanced!) they continue to function in the army essentially as they have for centuries: as cheerful noise-producing instruments to give a cadence for marching or as prescribed appurtenances of military ceremonies. The military band still exists too in the academic football band, now generally known as the "marching" band to distinguish it from the concert band which has no connection with the athletic program. The school "marching" band is a true military band; it is purely functional, and its problems are not those of the concert band. The schools for the most part recognize this distinction both in practice and in nomenclature; in some cases the two organizations are entirely separate, with different personnel and different training. In the army, conversely, there are a few large wind bands which are now almost entirely sedentary, and which, except for the fact that their personnel consists of sergeants, corporals and privates, can hardly be aptly described as "military" bands. The military band is best so classified by function rather than by clothing. Sousa's Band invariably wore uniforms of the semimilitary type, though Sousa himself and all his musicians were civilians and the band was an outstanding example of what should be called a concert band. The survival of the military tradition is still strong in that respect. The Goldman Band, when first organized in 1911, was briefly known as the New York Military Band. When it appeared in white summer suits, a disappointed lady was heard to observe that the band couldn't be much good: it couldn't even afford uniforms!

The concert band has in common with the orchestra the fact that it has the performance of music as its first purpose. That and the fact that it borrows much of the orchestra's music are about all the two have in common. Most people have a vague idea of the difference between the orchestra and the band, but it is not as a rule clearly understood. The general idea is that an orchestra has violins, which the band hasn't, and that the band has more cornets and other loud brass instruments. The fact is that the instrumental compositions of band and orchestra are greatly different, the orchestra not alone being based on a choir of stringed instruments, but being essentially a string choir plus wind instruments in variable numbers and dispositions. The band is a group of wind instrument players, approximating the orchestra in size, but with a disposition of instruments resembling nothing in the orchestra. There is no basic choir; the band is neither a brass choir with added woodwinds nor a reed choir with added brass. All compasses and registers are covered in the band, to the extent of which wind instruments are capable, and the band is sufficiently developed to be able to perform relatively complex music with full harmony and articulation of parts.

It is incorrect, strictly speaking, to say that the band is composed entirely of wind instruments. The band always has had a well-developed percussion section, often an overdeveloped one, a carry-over from the military again, where the emphasis was on functional time-beating for marching, and excessive cymbal-swatting for noise. According to current practice, the band may also include some stringed instruments. The use of the string bass and the harp is general, and the violoncello is now occasionally added.

The differences between the band and the

orchestra are the result of entirely different histories and different usages. The instrumental composition of the band is the outgrowth of utilitarian improvisation; that of the orchestra is the product of several centuries of conscious art. In the next chapter we shall examine the history of the band more extensively; we have, however, already mentioned that the band provides music for parades, that it once accompanied troops in movement, in short, that it needed mobility and had to produce sufficient volume to be heard outdoors. For this type of need, stringed instruments are completely impractical; not only are they too weak, even in masses, but the larger ones cannot be played at all while marching. These functional matters are of the greatest importance. The band never existed purely for the purpose of making music; it invariably was formed and made music for some specific need or occasion. It is only recently that the idea of the band as a purely independent and self-justifying medium has come to be accepted, and even now that acceptance is based on an adaptation of specific functions, however modified or outmoded.

The orchestra, on the other hand, has been shaped by composers, and composers are the most important of musicians. The versatility of stringed instruments was at an early date greater than that of any wind instrument, and it is natural that composers should base their instrumental writing on those instruments capable of the greatest range, flexibility and variety of expression. Other instruments were used as they became practical for serious purposes; Gabrieli's magnificent ensembles for trombones being a still too little-known case in point. The composer took what instruments he found useful and appropriate, and wrote for them. The important thing is that the composer *specified* what instruments he himself wished, or heard in his mind's ear, sometimes even scoring for instruments which he knew would not be available in performance. Bach sometimes wrote in this fashion, filling the parts of the absent instruments at the organ. The specification of instruments is always an expression of *intention* on the part of the composer, and it has always been the responsibility of musicians to execute these intentions as completely as possible. Composers have added instruments to the orchestra as they have become perfect enough to serve serious intentions, and as the choir of stringed instruments was complete at a fairly early date, it follows that most additions made by composers to the orchestra have been wind instruments. *Grove's Dictionary,* as a result, makes the untenable assertion that the "orchestra is becoming a large wind band plus strings." The orchestra may *look* like a large wind band surrounded by pathetic violinists, but it is still fundamentally a string choir, not because of numerical proportions, but because composers write for it as an orchestra and not as for a band plus strings.

The importance of the composer's role cannot possibly be overestimated. The development of bands illustrates the point negatively. Bands *had* to be made up of wind instruments from the beginning in order to be functional. The composer had to write for whatever was there, and if, as was usually the case, the band combination failed to interest him, he wrote for other combinations which did. The band then had to take some existing music and tailor it to fit its instrumentation. Aside from the fact that composers get tired of writing fanfares and marches, there was a very definite limit to the musical range of wind instrument combinations. They could not be tuned very well together; their timbres were no doubt often individually and collectively unpleasant; the bands could not therefore play for audiences who might be interested in serious musical expression. Later, as new wind instruments became more versatile and more reliable, they were added to bands in a rather haphazard manner. At one time or another, not excepting the present, nearly anything into which one can blow has been added to the band, and the music has had to be arranged or beaten about so that these combinations of instruments could play it. Here, clearly, it is the composer who comes off second best. Bands formed on this basis could never execute the expressed intentions of a composer, but since the instrumentation was the thing that came first, could only take those intentions and translate them into terms of convenience.

As a result, people who took composers seriously (that is, all people taking music seriously) quite reasonably developed feelings toward the band ranging from indifference to fright. The band, with its limited vocabulary, and in its useful and rightful place as a military or ambulatory body, found an audience only among the musically unsophisticated. Playing out of doors, as it invariably did, it was heard by large numbers of people who had never heard of composers. It has ever since played for the most part to the same sort of people, relying upon a repertory consisting, on the one hand, of popular and utilitarian music, with an immediate mass appeal, and, on the other, of translations of popularly accepted "composed" music to provide an illusion of artistic endeavor. We shall later examine the extent to which this has changed.

The band is still, in many respects, more similar to the popular dance orchestra than it is to the symphony orchestra. It is, despite its technical, numerical and even musical growth, still a phenomenon of "popular" music. To an extent, the band duplicates the dance orchestra in its emphasis on the arrangement of the music rather than on the composer of the music or on the music itself. Twenty dance orchestras will play the same piece twenty different ways, and the appeal of the performance will be in each case almost entirely based on the arrangement. This situation is not, of course, quite literally true of bands, especially today, but it is a closer approximation of the fact than most band enthusiasts like to admit. A performance by a band of a Beethoven overture may be any one of a number of things to a person who has never heard of Beethoven or listened to his music, but to a musical person it is an unauthorized version of a familiar work, and its acceptability (if the principle of transcription is admitted) will be judged on the basis of the arrangement. Whatever the merits of the performance, it is not what Beethoven wrote or intended; whether or not Beethoven himself would approve can no longer be determined. (This is of course to an extent true of some Beethoven performances by symphony orchestras, but there, at least, one assumes that the intention is to play what the composer wrote.)

The band today can give a good performance of nearly anything in the technical or artistic range of composition. It is no longer hampered by primitive instruments or restricted to playing at parades and drills. It has a variety of timbre, an extensive pitch range and controllable dynamics. It can be trained to play in tune and to respond to a conductor. To that extent it resembles the symphony orchestra. The differences nevertheless still remain greater and more important; they reside, even more than in the difference in instrumentation, in *what* the band plays and, as a consequence, *for whom* it plays.

The basic item of the band's repertory, and the only musical form that belongs to it by tradition, is the March. But here again, it is necessary to qualify the term, and to limit "march" in this sense to military march or quickstep. Grand Marches, or ceremonial marches, have in general been written for orchestra. The military march is the band's own. Nearly all of the remainder of the music it plays is transcribed or arranged from the literature of the piano or the orchestra, with some borrowings from other sources. It is absurd to claim that orchestra music sounds as good when played by a band; band men often make this claim, though they are the first to insist that a march can never sound like much of anything when played by an orchestra. It is true that much orchestra music sounds decently acceptable in a good band arrangement, and it is even true that some orchestra or piano pieces make excellent band numbers. Virgil Thomson remarks in one of his essays that he finds Wagner's music on the whole more satisfactory in band versions, though this may be a discreetly roundabout way of saying that he has no affection for Wagner's music. The band, for the most part, concentrates on the lighter "classics," works which have worn out their welcomes in the concert halls. There is certainly ample reason for playing many favorites which otherwise would not receive any hearing; but few works today fall into such disuse, with phonograph records available, with wired music in restaurants and public places, and countless radio orchestras batting out "semiclassics" (or perhaps "quadri-classics"). The radio feeds its audience a constant diet of "favorites," a diet so unvaried that many of the old favorites are finally becoming indigestible.

The tendency of many concert bands has been, while continuing to play the "lighter classics," to absorb larger and more elaborate portions of the orchestral repertory. Arguments for and against this practice have equally vociferous proponents. It is sufficient to note here that the practice of performing music from other literatures is general; it is, in fact, necessary if the band is to give concerts at all, for the band's own serious music is still insufficient to keep a good professional band in programs for even part of a season. The repertory of music specially written for band is, however, steadily growing, and, with more and more significant composers finding in the band a medium for reaching a new mass audience, this repertory should in time assume important proportions.

Of late years bandmasters have shown an inclination to reach out into less explored realms, and to vary the fare of favorite overtures and operatic selections with revivals of interesting music which has been neglected by the orchestras. This tendency is obviously one which should be encouraged, as it not only increases the value of the band as a musical and educational medium but also weakens the argument that the radio and other mass mediums can altogether assume the cultural functions of the band. Much old music, in particular, must be transcribed for modern performance (the performance of harpsichord music on a piano is an obvious and commonplace example), and there is no reason why much of this music should not sound as well for band as for any other type of ensemble. By performing this type of music, the band becomes a needed custodian of musical treasures which would otherwise tend to disappear.

For another large part of its characteristic program material, as band concerts are now presented, the band chooses from a variety of specially composed music, much of which bears the same relation to serious art as the soap-opera bears to high drama. What one cannot gainsay is that the soap-opera has a lot of listeners, and there is no need to belabor the point. Not all of this characteristic music is on that level: some of it has a special charm and uniqueness; it is music of a sort which has no place other than in the band concert. Included in this type of offering is the cornet solo, the appeal of which apparently remains as great as ever. There is also a certain style of music (in which class I would place most light opera music and such items as the "1812" Overture) which seems to be improved when it is performed out of doors.

The people who attend band concerts are the largest factor in determining the extent to which the band concentrates on this characteristic music or on any other kind of music. The band and its audience influence each other, to be sure. The band has introduced many people to music (both performers and listeners) and has stimulated their desires to expand their musical experiences and increase their musical pleasures. It is not the dish for those whose favorite form of music is the string quartet, although many serious musicians have taken pleasure in the vigor and brilliance of good band music. The band plays for a mass audience of extremely mixed taste. It gives delight to the musically unsophisticated and has a tremendous place in popular affection. It is a splendid form of community organization because it reaches great numbers of people in an immediate way, and because it is democratic enough in tradition to be closer to the people than any other type of large instrumental ensemble.

The band is an excellent musical organization for the community also because it affords a means for participation in music. Since the wind instruments are more easily learned than the strings, the band is the amateur organization par excellence. The amateur band, and this includes the thousands of school bands in the United States, is important not so much for the music it performs as for the participation in music which it makes possible. Having many people play instruments in an ensemble, instead of passively listening, is an eminently desirable goal, for playing an instrument is not only rewarding in itself but is the greatest real step toward the development of musical appreciation and understanding.

Thus the band has a variety of functions which, taken together, give it a special and individual place. It is capable of performing fine music well and of exerting great influence for good from a cultural and educational viewpoint, since it is essentially a popular institution. It is not comparable in make-up or function to the symphony orchestra, nor does it compete for the same kind of musical attention. The sooner that notion is forgotten the better for the realization of the band's own possibilities. The band should be evaluated neither too high nor too low in the scheme of musical activities. If it is not a competitor of the orchestra, neither is it a poor relation. It is a valid medium of musical expression in its own right, with a hold on the popular imagination which can be developed in important directions. The band has demonstrated its artistic capacities, which can, with awakened interest on the part of composers and a conscientious discharge of their musical responsibilities on the part of bandmasters, be still further exploited to assure the band of even greater claims to serious attention.

CHAPTER II

The Development of the Band: Origins and Functions

AT AN EARLY DATE in the development of European music nearly all mixed ensembles of instruments were called bands. The differentiation between band and orchestra, as we commonly accept them today, came about gradually; no clear line can be drawn until approximately the latter part of the seventeenth century. Until that time "band," as a generic term, covers the combinations of instruments employed by kings and nobles, assembled for court or municipal ceremonies, or used in theatrical performances of the time. The instrumental combinations occasionally found in the sixteenth century appear strange, and perhaps even unreasonable, to persons accustomed to the conventional orchestra and band of the twentieth century, yet they were no more odd than many of the combinations found in present-day dance or swing orchestras.

Certainly there was no attempt to regularize the constitution of instrumental groups in the sixteenth century. Purely instrumental music, that is, music excluding the human voice, was in general of secondary importance, and remained so until the eighteenth century. A good deal of the instrumental music was "occasional" music for performance at secular ceremonies and festivities, or, as we shall see, functional music in connection with civic or military activities. The composers of the sixteenth century wrote principally for the voice, assigning to instruments the secondary role of accompaniment, reinforcement or embroidery. The written instrumental music which we know was designed almost entirely for small units of related instruments, of which the "consort of viols," or an ensemble of lutes or recorders, is typical. The larger instrumental ensembles had little or no composed music; their music consisted for the most part of popular airs and dances, which were probably not performed from written notes. Although Henry VIII and Queen Elizabeth maintained enormous court "bands," * it is unlikely that any very large number of players ever performed simultaneously. The large assemblages of court musicians were maintained partly in order to have a large variety of instruments available, and partly for sheer prestige. For actual performances, the musicians were probably divided into small ensembles; the serious instru-

* Queen Elizabeth's ensemble in 1587 consisted of 16 trumpets, 6 sackbuts, a bagpipe, 8 viols, 2 rebecks, as well as a number of virginals, lutes and harps. Henry VIII's "band" was similar, but bigger.

mental music of the court was certainly played by viols, lutes and recorders (although we must not forget the wonderful keyboard music of the time), with the trumpets and fifes, and of course the bagpipe, reserved for fanfares and general noisemaking on special occasions.

The small unit of related instruments was the typical ensemble of the sixteenth century and continued to be dominant through the seventeenth. The string quartet is our most direct inheritance from that period. It would appear that the esthetic ideal of the serious music of that time was homogeneity of sound, rather than diversity and contrast as we experience it in modern orchestration. The choir of human voices is the most perfect example of blended tonal quality, and it is in writing for voices that the highest expression of sixteenth and seventeenth century music is attained. The serious writing for instruments reflects the desires of composers for unity of timbre; it was differentiated from vocal style to a certain extent by its greater rhythmic and intervallic complexity (although there is argument on this point among musicologists), but "instrumentation" as such was certainly an alien conception. The great instrumental music of seventeenth century Europe is represented by the "consort of viols" in England, the sonorous *sonate* and *canzone* for trombones in Italy, and on a more popular level, by the four- and five-part music written for *zinken* and trombones in Germany.

It is true that one can find examples of mixed instrumentation, but they appear to be exceptions. The modern conception of "orchestration" or instrumentation does not appear much before 1700. Giovanni Gabrieli (1557–1612) composed a few works in which he indicated mixed scoring, and we have "broken consorts" by Morley and other English composers. Opera, which arose as a new art form at the very beginning of the seventeenth century, began to involve orchestration, as in Monteverde, which was sometimes of considerable originality and elaborateness. For purely instrumental music, however, the string choir became the basis on which the large forms were developed.

The band as we know it today may be said to stem partly from the fifes, drums and trumpets associated with European courts and armies, and partly from the ensemble of similar instruments used for secular music in the sixteenth and seventeenth centuries. It is the eventual modification and merging of these two usages that resulted in the prototype of the military band. The development from the early martial use of trumpets and drums is easy enough to trace. If the use of instruments to signal charges is out of date, the idea of music to inspire troops is still, at least in principle, tenable. Actual military signaling by means of trumpets goes back at least to the thirteenth century, and survives today in the bugle calls for reveille, taps, assembly and other routines. An Italian treatise of the sixteenth century, speaking of the military usages of the time, observes that "an army would not attack the enemy unless summoned by the sound of trumpet or drum." (An obvious way of avoiding war would apparently have been to exterminate all trumpet players and drummers.) Trumpet and drum music during the course of the sixteenth and seventeenth centuries appears to have been confined to signals and flourishes; the rudimentary military marches and tunes of the period were performed by the more versatile fifes or bagpipes, in combination with drums. The two usages, signaling and marching, seem to have constituted the extent of military music until the latter part of the seventeenth century.

An important feature of the military music of the time was the separation of instruments according to type and tradition as well as function. Thus trumpets came to be associated with the cavalry, as did kettle-drums; while bagpipes and fifes were characteristic of the foot-soldiery. The trumpet, from earliest times until the period of Bach, was reserved for special uses and was in general considered an appurtenance of the nobility. Thus it could never be used in combination with more plebeian instruments, such as the zinke

A rare photograph of the United States Marine Band (37 players), under its most famous leader. Note the seating of the cornets in the old style, immediately at the conductor's right, and the placing of the horns in the front row center. *From the collection of Edwin Franko Goldman, Mt. Tremper, N. Y.*

A contemporary lithograph of Gilmore's Band, depicted either before or after a performance of the Anvil Chorus. *From the collection of Edwin Franko Goldman, Mt. Tremper, N. Y.*

or cornett, the sackbut or trombone, or the pipes and fifes. The precise social distinctions are a bit hard to draw at this distance; it appears that it was permissible to use trumpets in combination with horns (that is, the prototype of the horn, known as the *buccina*) in cavalry bands, but not elsewhere. It is, however, to be noted that the distinction between the horn and the trumpet of the period was not great, both having more resemblance to our bugle than to any other modern instrument. Cavalry bands were thus composed of trumpets and horns, with kettledrums, and retained this composition until fairly recent times. These bands are more truly the prototype of the present bugle corps than of the military or concert band. The distinction between cavalry music and infantry music was maintained throughout the nineteenth century and well into the twentieth.

Of the remaining available instruments in the sixteenth and seventeenth centuries, the bagpipe came to the fore for infantry music, as it undoubtedly made more noise than the recorder, the cornett or the sackbut. It must never be forgotten that in military music, and in outdoor music generally, noise is a primary object. It has not been generally observed that Lully, in using bands of oboes for the military music of Louis XIV, was perpetuating a bagpipe tradition for infantry music. These oboe ensembles, organized about the middle of the seventeenth century by Lully as regimental bands to form a part of the regular army, were the first regularly constituted military bands of which we have record. The marches which Lully composed or arranged for these bands are among our earliest surviving examples of written band music. The pieces are all in four parts, with drums. The oboes of Lully's time (descendants of shawms, pommers, and other double reeds of great antiquity) were of all sizes from treble to bass, and would be roughly comparable to oboes, English horns and bassoons.* In using one type of instrument, in this case a double-reed, Lully was not only conforming to the best traditions of making plenty of noise, but at the same time to the established usage of keeping different instruments separate.

This phase of instrumental usage also characterized the civil, or municipal, music of the sixteenth and seventeenth centuries, which, just as much as the military music, helped determine the character of the band of today. Many towns, especially in Germany and Austria, took great pride in official or semiofficial municipal music, made by performers who were civil functionaries. The duties of these players, going back to medieval custom, were originally to announce the hours by musical signals from the towers in which they kept watch. It was inevitable that these simple

* A more detailed discussion of this point, and of other instruments mentioned in this chapter, will be found in Chapter V.

functions should be expanded. By the middle of the sixteenth century, they were playing chorales from their towers and providing, on the street level, music for festivals, state occasions and weddings. A function which they early assumed was that of accompanying chorales at church services.

The instruments on which these *thuermer,* or towermen, performed were trombones and zinken, or cornetts, wooden instruments with cup mouthpieces. Cornetts had finger holes, much like recorders, and could play all notes within a compass of two octaves. They could thus perform any type of melody, whereas the trumpet and horn were of course restricted to fanfares. It was considered that the cornett and the trombone were related instruments in character and sound quality, although the trombone belongs to the trumpet family and the cornett to the horns.* (Here again we are faced with the problem of why the trumpet was a "reserved" instrument while the trombone was not.) In the sixteenth and seventeenth centuries trombones were constructed in several sizes, from bass to descant, while at least four sizes of cornett were in common use. Thus a complete choir of

* The reader is cautioned against confusing the ancient cornett (zinke or *cornetto*) with the modern cornet. The old cornett must be considered as a horn, although it was made of wood. The forerunners of many modern "brasses" were made of ivory or other materials. Many of the functions, though not the structure or appearance, of the ancient cornetto have been inherited by the modern cornet or fluegelhorn.

each instrument was available, and there has come down to us music written for choirs of cornetts alone or for trombones alone.

These little bands of tower musicians were in many real senses the precursors of the civilian concert bands we know today. Their functions, if not their instrumentation, were identical. They provided the popular outdoor music, the marches for town festivities and ceremonies, and the accompaniments for community singing. It is from these groups that the *popular* (as opposed to the *military*) aspect of band music stems. From the military, the town band later absorbed the trumpet and drum, just as the military band in turn absorbed the trombone and the instruments which began to emerge in the eighteenth century.

Before we proceed to the emergence of the eighteenth century band, combining the military and town bands, it will be interesting to examine a little more closely the nature of the wind instruments we have been discussing, and to make some further observations concerning their development. We have seen that the cavalry band used trumpets and horns; these were natural instruments, having no holes or keys, but producing only the notes in the harmonic series. These instruments were therefore suited by their limitations to be used together. Their musical efforts could in no case achieve effects more varied than that of more or less elaborate fanfares.

Cornetts and trombones, on the other hand, could produce all chromatic intervals within their ranges, the trombone by virtue of the slide and the cornett by means of finger holes. Thus, the two sets of instruments were separated not so much by their tonal qualities (although the cornett and trumpet differed very greatly) as by their capacities. Trumpet music, being of a rudimentary character, was as a rule learned by ear, and handed down without notation. Music for cornetts and trombones, however, early developed something of a serious character. Besides the chorales and popular pieces which could be played by these combinations, a literature was specifically written for them by composers of the period. By the latter part of the seventeenth century, this literature had assumed respectable proportions,* and it is to be presumed that the tradition of playing from written notes had become fairly established.

The selection, or rather the evolution, of these groups of instruments must have resulted as the necessity of creating some order out of the profusion of wind instruments became obvious. We have early accounts of gatherings of players upon the most in-

* For material on this wind instrument music, the reader is referred to my book, *The Band's Music.*

credibly varied types of sound producers, on which occasions all played a melody in unison or octaves. The problem of co-ordinating the pitches does not seem to have received serious attention or, if it did, it may have been abandoned in despair. There was no mass production of instruments, nor any agreement as to the correct number of vibrations for middle C, in any case. Probably, too, the timbres of the many types of instruments fought with one another in a manner calculated to distress the ears of the most insensitive. It is, in fact, barely possible that the primary object of noise was not only attained, but exceeded. In short, the mixed gathering of instruments more than likely resulted in almost anything but a concord of sound.

Whether the practice of using related instruments avoided many of the difficulties of intonation is difficult to say, but at least the mixture of sometimes irreconcilable timbres and harmonic series could be avoided. Presumably it was possible to find "matched sets" of schalmeys, or cornetts, or recorders, capable of performing in accurate pitch relation one to another. That step once achieved, the elimination from ensembles of instruments incapable of tuning or blending soon followed. Those instruments were retained which not only could perform together but also belonged to families including all the ranges, from treble to bass, which are found in the human voice.

One immense advantage of stringed instruments for ensemble playing obviously resides in the fact that they can easily be tuned. It was therefore possible to mass large numbers of stringed instruments at almost any stage of their development.* This could not have been true of cornetts, schalmeys, pommers, recorders or any of the other myriad types of wind instruments. The effect on the ears of Louis XIV's band of oboes is perhaps best left unimagined. We do not know how many double reeds were actually employed in these bands, but it is safe to assume that the greater the doubling of the parts the more shattering the noise would have been. The only wind instruments that were safe to use in fairly large masses were the trombones, which, then as now, were capable of the most accurate pitch adjustment. It is in these terms that one can explain the use by many composers of large numbers of trombones, in many choirs, while in the same period cornetts and other wind instruments were used only in groups of four or five. In other words, there was a practical top limit to the number of wind instruments one could reasonably use with any expectation of obtaining a semblance of tuning. This is perhaps one of the reasons why orchestras began to develop along more elaborate lines at a time

* The art of violinmaking in fact reached its highest perfection in the seventeenth century.

when wind bands were still restricted to small groups of players on one type of instrument.

We do not, for our purposes, have to follow in detail the development of orchestration in the hands of Monteverde, Bach, Handel and Haydn, for this development had little direct effect on the formation of the wind band. Its negative effect was to relegate the wind ensemble to a much lower status, musically and socially, than it had enjoyed before. We find no wind instrument music in the early eighteenth century comparable in beauty or seriousness to the sonate or canzone of Gabrieli, or even to the tower music of Reiche and Pezel. The tower musicians themselves disappeared in about 1715. The band or wind ensemble became more and more restricted to frankly popular and military use, as the emphasis in "art" music shifted from the vocal part-writing style to an independent instrumental music of too great complexity for wind instrument performance.

This period was marked by the development of certain wind instruments and the disappearance of others. The *chalumeau,* or clarinet, was greatly improved in 1690 by J. C. Denner of Nuremberg, and was in fairly common use by about 1720. The cornett and trombone fell into disuse with the improvement of the horn and bassoon at about the same time. As a result, the instrumentation of the town and military bands assumed an informal character, as the older instruments disappeared and newer ones, in various stages of development, were adopted. The new instruments came to the fore primarily as orchestral instruments, with techniques and timbres evolved through use in orchestral scores. The new musical style included the idea of combined timbres and alternations of contrasting instruments. We do not have complete documentation for all the steps in the evolution of the instrumental grouping of the wind ensembles of the early eighteenth century, but we know that by the middle of the century the characteristic ensemble was an octet of 2 oboes, 2 clarinets, 2 bassoons and 2 horns. To these eight instruments were sometimes added one or two flutes, a serpent,* and of course various drums. This type of band, common in England, France, Austria and Germany, was officially approved by Frederick the Great in 1763 as the standard for the Prussian infantry. An odd type of "military band" of the period was that of Spain, which in 1769 consisted of 2 fifes, 2 clarinets, and drums. This band was, however, a more direct descendant of the earlier military bands than the more sophisticated octet, which definitely shows the influence of the orchestral writing of the period.

Haydn, Karl Philipp Emanuel Bach and Mozart,

* The serpent, used well into the nineteenth century, is the bass of the cornett or zinke family, a large wooden instrument with six finger holes, played with a cup mouthpiece. It was curved so that the player could manage to cover the finger holes; hence the name.

among others, did in fact write occasional pieces for just such combinations of wind instruments. Some of this music was specifically designed to be played out of doors, and may certainly be considered authentic band music. There are even a few marches among these little works. It is possible that these were played, along with the traditional military marches and popular airs, by some of the regimental bands of the time.

The trumpet lost its "reserved" character and appeared in the infantry band during the eighteenth century. Various percussion instruments, such as the cymbals and the triangle, were adopted as a result of the vogue of the Turkish Janizary bands. Other instruments, too, were added, but in an irregular way. Thus contra bassoons occasionally appear instead of serpents, and one finds occasional mention of basset horns. Trombones were used hardly at all; they were apparently considered to be related in character to the cornett, and when the latter instrument fell into disuse, the trombone was carried with it. It is not until about 1790 that trombones are again mentioned in connection with military bands. Although Handel knew and used the trombone (as did Mozart), it is recorded that great difficulty was experienced in finding sackbuts and players for the great Handel Commemoration in London in 1784.

Toward the end of the eighteenth century, public band concerts in the open air were an established institution in all the capitals of Europe. Bands had begun to grow in size, and an air of international rivalry over them had begun to make itself felt. The expenses of maintaining bands were in some cases assumed by the state instead of by the commanding officers, as had been the rule previously. In 1762, Marshal Biron persuaded Louis XV to authorize army bands of sixteen men at public expense. These bands were simply double octets, with four each of oboes, clarinets, horns and bassoons, instead of two. One of the celebrated regimental bands in England, that of the Royal Artillery, was founded in the same year, with eight players.

Public concerts by military bands first became common in Germany, where the tower musicians had established a tradition of popular outdoor music. An eighteenth century account tells us that "it was the custom in all the garrison towns in Germany for the band to play a few numbers each evening before retreat" and that this custom not only gave great pleasure to the inhabitants of the town, but that "the relations between the citizens and the soldiers were greatly improved thereby." The custom, in any case, soon spread from Germany to France and other countries. The same account tells us that in Paris the Band of the Gardes Françaises "gave serenades on the boulevards . . . this was the rendez-vous à la mode." In 1777, this same band gave open-air concerts at Versailles, at which the public was permitted to mix with the court. It is recorded that several of the foreign diplomats, including Mercy-Argenteau, the ambassador of Maria Theresa, viewed with great alarm this admission of the common people.

Vienna, too, had public concerts, and at least one band which, by 1781, had come to consist of 11 players. To the usual octet had been added a trumpet, a side drum and a bass drum. This combination is interesting as being one of the first to include percussion for any other than purely military purposes. Quite the largest band up to that time was assembled in 1782, when a grand concert was given at the Trianon in honor of the visit of the Grand Duke Paul of Russia. For this occasion the Gardes Françaises Band was augmented by 36 musicians from the Swiss Guards.

Regimental and national rivalry led to the rapid growth in size of bands in all countries. In 1783, the Duke of York introduced a band of 12 players imported from Germany for the Coldstream Guards. This band included 2 oboes, 4 clarinets, 2 horns, 2 bassoons, 1 trumpet, and 1 serpent. This was obviously a huge and impressive affair in comparison with the bands then usual. Trombones and percussion in the Turkish style were added some years later, making this one of the earliest of "modern" military bands.

It must be remembered that orchestral music of

the eighteenth century had prepared the way for the enlargement of bands. Composers of symphonies had increased the size of the orchestra, and by the demands of their music had made necessary new techniques of ensemble playing. Most of the instruments had been improved so that erratic elements of performance were much reduced, and although the trumpets and horns were still limited to natural notes, the technique of using instruments in different pitches, or of altering pitch by means of crooks, had been evolved to minimize these limitations.

Just when the clarinet came to the fore and replaced the oboe as the primary soprano voice of the band is difficult to say with accuracy. (It is interesting to note that military bandsmen in the early eighteenth century were all known as "oboists," from the predominance of that instrument.) A military march score in my possession, dated 1795, and scored for twelve instruments, has the melody generally in the oboes, although it is taken up occasionally by the clarinets. As the most conservative conclusion, one would have to state that the instruments were then of equal importance, with the oboe somewhat more prominent. Kastner and Kappey, however, note the complete absence of the oboe in the bands of the French Republic of the same year, giving the instrumentation as 1 flute, 6 clarinets, 3 bassoons, 2 horns, 1 trumpet, 1 serpent, and drums. Fétis's account of a typical band of the period also establishes the priority of the clarinet, although the instrumentation he gives includes oboes as well. The band, according to Fétis, included 1 piccolo, 2 oboes, 4 clarinets, 2 bassoons, 2 horns and 3 drums. On all the evidence, it would certainly be safe to assert that by the beginning of the nineteenth century the clarinet had clearly established its place as the leading voice of the band's woodwinds.

It is evident that by the latter part of the eighteenth century the military band had assumed the functions of the town band and of the old tower musicians. It had gradually evolved from a private ensemble, hired by a regimental officer for his own pleasure and prestige, to a semipublic institution which provided music for the people at large. Concerts by military bands were some slight evidence of the demand for democratization in the arts and in society. Band music was still, however, clearly limited in its scope, and was certainly not a concern of serious musicians.

The development of the band was more profoundly influenced by the French Revolution than by any event before or since. In the great surges of popular enthusiasm which marked the establishment of a new order, music was a vital outlet of expression.

Bands, organized for and by the people, and grown to a size never before known, occupied an important place in the patriotic celebrations and open-air festivals. The number of these demonstrations, and the abundance of new music written for them, testify to the emotional fervor of the first years of the Republic. In 1789, a young musician named Sarrette gathered 45 wind instrument players from existing bands and orchestras, and formed the band of the National Guard. This band was augmented to 70 * players in 1790, and was supported by the city of Paris. Gossec (1734–1829), the leading French composer of the time, became bandmaster, with Charles Simon Catel (1773–1830), another celebrated composer, as his assistant. The National Guard Band, dissolved by decree of the Convention in 1792, became the nucleus of the famous National Conservatory of Music in Paris, and its place in French musical history is a distinguished one.

Other large bands flourished, and all the leading composers of the time provided them with new music. From the standpoint of spontaneous activity, popularity and importance, the period was perhaps the most exciting and significant in the history of band music. A leading scholar of the period, in describing the status of the revolutionary bands, writes that "the

* 78, according to one scholar (C. V. D. Pierre).

progress was considerable, due to the initiative of the musicians of the National Guard of Paris, the founders of the Conservatory. Breaking with all precedent, these artists used every known wind instrument in the military bands, which had theretofore been composed simply of oboes, clarinets, horns and bassoons. They even invented new instruments. Furthermore, they enlarged and strengthened the repertory with original compositions, varied in instrumentation, and cast in the form of concert overtures and symphonies, more highly developed, and obviously more interesting, than the potpourris on light-opera airs which up to that time had formed the larger part of the military band repertory." These compositions, including splendid works by Gossec, Cherubini, Méhul, Lesueur, Catel and others, are unfortunately almost unknown among contemporary bandsmen.

Under Napoleon, the great activity in composition for the wind band dwindled, although there are some interesting specimens of marches written by Paisiello, Paër and Cherubini. The last-named served for a time as bandmaster of the National Guard, and received from Napoleon a decoration in acknowledgment of his services. The band of the National Guard, as well as the bands of other military and civic organizations, were reorganized and expanded. The bands of the Napoleonic armies were considered the finest then in existence, and served as models for those of all other countries of Europe. In 1809, according to Fétis, infantry bands of the French army were made up of 1 piccolo, 1 E*b* or F clarinet, 6 or 8 clarinets in B*b* or C, 2 horns, 2 bassoons, 1 trumpet, 2 or 3 trombones, 1 or 2 serpents, and 4 percussion players. Other historians state that these bands contained as many as 43 players. In any event, these bands clearly foreshadow the basic instrumentation of the modern concert band.

Evidence of the growth of the band in other countries is found in the score of Beethoven's Military March in D, written in 1816. This work calls for 2 piccolos, 2 oboes, 5 clarinets in C, 2 bassoons, 1 contra bassoon, 8 trumpets, 4 horns, 1 bass horn, 2 trombones, 1 serpent and percussion, or 32 players in all. In England, too, there were bands of comparable size. By 1812, the band of the Royal Artillery, which until 1792 had had only eight players, numbered 35, plus three Negro drummers. The latter were a great feature of many bands in the early nineteenth century.

It is instructive, after noting the general tendency toward the increase in size of bands, to compare the quite different constructions of bands in three countries of Europe in the third decade of the century. We shall have many occasions, from this time on, to remark upon the essentially *national* character of bands and band music. Typical bands of England, France and Austria in about 1825 were:

England (Royal Artillery Band)

2 flutes	3 key bugles *
3 oboes	3 trombones (alto, tenor, bass)
11 clarinets	1 ophicleide *
3 bassoons	2 serpents
2 horns	2 bass horns
2 trumpets	5 drums

Total: 39 players

France (Infantry Band)

2 flutes in F or E*b*	2 contra bassoons
2 clarinets in F or E*b*	2 trumpets, F or E*b*
4 oboes	4 horns, F or E*b*
12 clarinets, B*b* or C	2 trombones
6 bassoons	

Total: 36 players

Austria (Infantry Band)

1 piccolo, D*b*	2 key trumpets in E*b*
2 clarinets in A*b*	2 trumpets in A*b*
1 clarinet in E*b*	2 trumpets in E*b*
9 clarinets in B*b*	1 trumpet in F
1 bassoon	1 trumpet in C
1 serpent	1 bass trumpet in E*b*
2 horns in E*b*	2 tenor trombones
2 horns in A*b*	1 bass trombone
	1 side drum

Total: 32 players

* The key bugle was patented in 1810 by James Halliday, an Irish bandmaster, who devised a system of holes and covering keys which made it possible to play a complete scale on the wide-bore cavalry bugle. The ophicleide was the same instrument in principle, but pitched an octave lower

From this point on, the history of the wind band is one of constant experiment and enlargement. Even today, as we shall see, the band differs from country to country, and is still in the process of adopting and discarding a variety of instruments. Bandmasters have striven to find the best combination for the performance of music out of doors, for it is there that nearly all band concerts have taken place. Military demands and political economies have helped to determine the size and constitution of army bands, maintained as part of a nation's armed establishment. In this connection, it may be observed that the French bands of 1825, mentioned above, were reduced to 12 to 27 players only two years later, because of an official decision to effect economies.

One of the first important reformers who attempted to systematize the wind band was the German, Wilhelm Wieprecht (1802–1872) who, in about 1830, succeeded in persuading the Prussian military authorities to follow his recommendations for the instrumentation of cavalry and infantry bands. Wieprecht first proved the advantages of using trumpets and horns equipped with valves, which had been devised about 1813 and which enabled the player to produce all the notes of the chromatic scale without changing instruments or having to insert "crooks" of various lengths into the tubing. The distinction of being the first to apply valves to wind instruments is disputed among an Irishman named Claggett and two Germans, Bluehmel and Stoelzel, who seem to have arrived at the idea at about the same time. Wieprecht also used the key bugle, but as valves were perfected and proved to be infinitely more satisfactory, he abandoned this instrument about 1835.

The first experiment successfully concluded by Wieprecht was with a cavalry brass band. His instrumentation consisted of 2 soprano cornets in B*b*, 2 key bugles in B*b*, 2 alto cornets in E*b*, 8 trumpets in E*b*, 2 tenor horns in B*b*, 1 bass horn in B*b*, and 3 trombones in B*b*. The cornets, trumpets and horns were all fitted with valves, and many of them were designed by Wieprecht, who was an inventor and acoustician as well as a musician. This band obviously made all of its predecessors at once obsolete, and its success brought to Wieprecht a request to reform the infantry bands in the same decisive manner. The first infantry band so reformed had the following composition:

2 flutes
2 oboes
1 clarinet in A*b*
2 clarinets in E*b*
8 clarinets in B*b*
2 bassoons
2 contra bassoons
2 soprano cornets in E*b*
2 alto cornets in E*b*
4 trumpets
4 French horns
2 tenor horns in B*b*
2 tenor trombones
2 bass trombones
1 euphonium
4 bombardons (basses)
5 percussion

Total: 47 players

Wieprecht continued to experiment with the constitution of the wind band, and in 1845 suggested the following instrumentation, based on the comparative tonal strengths of the instruments. He divided the instruments into three classes: soft, medium and loud. I append this instrumentation as a curiosity, as it shows a novel approach to the problem of instrumental strength for playing in the open air.

Soft instruments:	2 flutes
	2 clarinets in A*b* or G
	2 clarinets in E*b* or D
	8 clarinets in B*b* or A
	2 oboes in E*b* or D
	2 bassoons
	2 batyphones (a sort of bass clarinet invented by Wieprecht)
Medium instruments:	2 cornets in B*b* or A
	2 cornets in E*b* or D
	2 tenor horns in B*b* or A
	1 baritone horn in B*b* or A
	2 bass horns in F or E*b*
Loud instruments:	4 trumpets in E*b* or D
	2 tenor trombones in B*b*
	2 bass trombones in F or E*b*
	2 bass tubas in F or E*b*
	3 percussion players
Total:	42 players

A younger contemporary of Wieprecht who also exerted a most important influence on the development of bands was Antoine Joseph Sax (1814–1894), better known as Adolphe Sax, a Belgian instrument maker who established himself in Paris in 1842. Aside from inventing the saxophone, an accomplishment by which he is most remembered, he created a new family of brass instruments, the saxhorns, and succeeded in having the bands of France reorganized in line with his recommendations. The saxhorns were not altogether new in principle, but were an application of a perfected valve system to the family of conical-bore brass instruments, with various modifications to correct the intonation and to give facility for playing in all keys. They ranged from the soprano bugle, or fluegelhorn, to the saxtuba, which in all essentials is still the orchestral tuba of today. The intermediate instruments, althorns, tenor horns, baritones and so on, are still used in military and concert bands, although they have never found a welcome in the orchestra.

Berlioz was one of Sax's earliest and most vociferous supporters, helping him even to the extent of organizing concerts featuring Sax's instruments. For one of these, in 1843, when the saxophone was still in the experimental stage, Berlioz wrote a sextet which unfortunately has been lost. This work was scored for very high trumpet in B*b*, a new cornet, bugle (fluegelhorn), clarinet, bass clarinet and saxophone. It was performed by six of the leading players of the time, including Arban (who played the bugle part) and Sax himself on the brand-new saxophone. Comettant, in his biography of Sax, relates that the saxophone was not quite finished on the day of the concert. "Sax, a man never discouraged by difficulties, tied the keys on with string, and held the other parts of the instrument together with sealing wax. Berlioz himself conducted the new work. After a loud *tutti,* which filled the hall with a powerful but gentle sound, each player had a skillfully written solo passage which showed the advantages of his instrument. The last and most important passage was for the saxophone. A long-held note was conspicuously featured near the end of this solo. Sax played this note with great calm and assurance, swelling and diminishing the sound, giving it every nuance possible. He had forgotten the fingering of the next note, and kept going in order to gain time. Finally his memory came back, just as his lungs were about exhausted. The passage ended, and the audience burst into enthusiastic applause: it appeared to the listeners that this very long holding of the note was proof of immense skill, and a bold and happy instrumental inspiration. The concert was a genuine triumph for the inventor."

The saxophone was patented in 1846, and as it is an instrument familiar to everyone, it is not necessary to describe it here. The effect of its introduction, however, along with that of the saxhorns, was immense on the bands of the time. For a period all oboes, bassoons and horns disappeared from French military bands, and the number of clarinets decreased considerably, as Sax's instruments replaced them. Since Sax was an instrument manufacturer, he was perhaps less interested in the tonal balance of the band than he was in selling the authorities as many of his products as possible. For a time, he enjoyed what was almost a monopoly on providing instruments for all the official military bands, a fact which may be cited in support of the contention that the development of bands has often been influenced by non-musical considerations. In 1845, a jury of celebrated French musicians decided on the following official instrumentation for French infantry bands, not going quite as far as Sax wished, but retaining many of his suggestions:

1 piccolo in C	1 soprano saxhorn in E*b*
1 clarinet in E*b*	2 saxhorns in B*b*
14 clarinets in B*b*	2 alto saxhorns in E*b*
2 bass clarinets	3 tenor saxhorns in B*b*
2 saxophones	4 contrabass saxhorns in E*b*
4 French horns	1 valve trombone
2 cornets	2 slide trombones
2 trumpets	2 ophicleides
	5 percussion players

Total: 50 players

Although the saxophone and most of the sax-horns established themselves as permanent components of all military and concert bands since their introduction, few bands have ever used them in the proportions advocated by their inventor. For a time, however, French bands seemed to be developing more along the lines of Sax's ideas than along those made official in 1845. A pamphlet on military bands written by Albert Perrin appeared in 1852 and caused the entire subject of band organization to be reopened. Perrin was a strong supporter of Sax, and publication of his pamphlet in English and Italian a few years later stimulated the reform of bands in both countries. In France, the results were immediate and far-reaching. The government issued a plan in 1854, making the following the official instrumentation of infantry bands:

2 flutes or piccolos
2 oboes
4 E*b* clarinets
8 B*b* clarinets
8 saxophones (2 each of sopranos, altos, tenors and baritones)
2 cornets, B*b*
4 trumpets, B*b*
2 E*b* soprano saxhorns (fluegelhorns)
2 B*b* saxhorns (fluegelhorns)
2 alto saxotrombas (E*b* altos)
2 B*b* baritones
4 bass saxhorns, B*b*
4 contrabasses, E*b* and BB*b*

3 tenor trombones
1 bass trombone
5 percussion
Total: 55

This instrumentation remained in effect but a comparatively short time, as both official decrees and practical usage re-established the clarinets in the position they held in all other European bands, which, although adopting Sax's instruments, followed more closely the models established by Wieprecht.

One further instrument of some importance made its appearance about 1863. This was the sarrusophone, a double-reed conical-bore instrument made of metal, invented by Sarrus, a bandmaster in the French army. Built like the saxophones and saxhorns, in various ranges from soprano to bass, it provided a complete family of instruments of a very penetrating timbre, designed to replace the oboe, English horn and bassoon for use in wind bands, and specifically for playing out of doors. (It will be remembered that Wieprecht classified oboes and bassoons as "soft" instruments.) Sarrusophones have been used, especially the bass, in some European bands, but their use has been infrequent in America and England. Many sarrusophones used together must produce an effect somewhat similar to that of Lully's oboe bands, or even to the bagpipes of an earlier day, and it may indeed be surmised that the sarrusophone more nearly approaches in quality the ancient oboe, or schalmey, than any modern instrument.

By 1850 or thereabouts, it may be said that the modern wind band had taken shape in all major respects. The variations in instrumentation were, and still are, considerable, but the purposes, organization and functions of wind bands were very much the same all over Europe. Band concerts were a regular feature of popular musical life, and military bands were to be heard in parks, at resorts and at public festivals. For those who may feel that the performance of "classical" music by wind bands is a relatively recent development, it should be noted that Wieprecht transcribed for band the Second, Third, Fifth, Seventh and Ninth Symphonies of Beethoven, in their entireties, as well as the *Battle* Symphony, two symphonies of Mozart and an enormous number of overtures and concert pieces by the "great" composers. In Wieprecht's time, well before the invention of radio or electrical amplification, these transcriptions had the very great merit of bringing much music to many people who would otherwise have remained unaware of its existence. This has always been one of the legitimate functions of the concert band as a popularizer of serious music.

An international band contest was held in Paris in 1867, and illustrates better than any other example the nature and status of European bands at that time. Nine countries sent bands: France, Prussia, Austria, Russia, Spain, Belgium, Baden, Holland and Bavaria. England was invited to participate, but permission for the Royal Artillery Band to make the trip was refused. Great interest was aroused in this festival and contest. The judges included Delibes, Ambroise Thomas, Félicien David, Hanslick, von Buelow and Georg Kastner. The bands averaged about 60 players each, by far the largest being that of Prussia, directed by Wieprecht. This band was composed of 85 players, and since it is larger than any we have noted so far, it will be interesting to detail its instrumentation:

4 flutes and piccolos
4 oboes (and English horn)
1 A*b* clarinet (sopranino)
4 E*b* or F clarinets
16 B*b* clarinets (8, 1st; 8, 2nd)
6 bassoons
4 contra bassoons
4 B*b* cornets
4 E*b* cornets (altos)
8 trumpets (in G, F, E*b*, E and D)
4 French horns
4 tenor horns
2 baritone horns
8 trombones
6 bass tubas
6 percussion

String basses were used by two of the bands taking part in the festival: those of Belgium and Holland, the latter having three of these instruments. This is the first example I have been able to find of the inclusion of stringed instruments in wind bands.

The contest itself took place on July 27, 1867, with each band playing the required work—Weber's *Oberon* Overture—and one piece of its own choice. The selections give so clear a picture of the band repertory of the time that I list them here in full:

Baden: Finale of *The Lorelei* ....Felix Mendelssohn
Spain: Fantasy on National Airs
Prussia: Fantasy on *The Prophet*........G. Meyerbeer
Austria: Overture, *William Tell* ....G. A. Rossini
Belgium: Potpourri on *William Tell*......G. A. Rossini
Bavaria: Introduction and Bridal Chorus
from *Lohengrin* ....Richard Wagner
Holland: Fantasy on *Faust* ....Charles Gounod
Paris Guards: Bridal Chorus and Wedding
March from *Lohengrin* ....R. Wagner
Russia: Fantasy on National Airs
Paris Guides: Fantasy on *The Carnival of Venice*

Needless to say, the contest ended with recriminations on all sides. First place was given to the bands of Prussia, Austria (conducted by Zimmermann) and the Paris Guards (conducted by Paulus), doubtless in order to avoid an international incident. Peace was kept at least to the extent of permitting a final festival concert a week later, with all bands except those of France participating. On that occasion the program was as follows:

Austria: Overture, *Der Freischuetz*.........von Weber
Torch Dance ....Meyerbeer
Baden: Finale of *The Lorelei* ....Mendelssohn
Overture, *The Marriage of Figaro* .....Mozart
Bavaria: *National* Overture ....Lindpaintner
Overture, *La Gazza Ladra* ....Rossini
Belgium: Overture, *Masaniello* ....Auber
Fantasy on *The Huguenots* ......Meyerbeer
Holland: Overture, *William Tell* ....Rossini
Fantasy on *Lohengrin* ....Wagner
Prussia: Polonaise from *Struensee*..........Meyerbeer
March from *Tannhaeuser* ....Wagner
Spain: Overture, *Etoile du Nord* ....Meyerbeer
Overture, *Raymond* ....Thomas
Russia: Fantasy on National Airs
Fantasy on *A Life for the Tsar*........Glinka

Nearly all the music played at this festival remains standard repertory of bands today, but I should like to comment on the amount of this music that was *contemporary* music when it was performed in 1867. None of it, however, had been written for band. The transcriptions must have varied considerably in merit; at least one of them aroused some comment at the time: the English horn solo in the *William Tell* Overture was performed by the fluegelhorn player of the Austrian band.

Although England was not represented by a band at this festival, band music had made immense progress in that country. By 1839, the band of the Royal Artillery included 48 players of whom, however, seven were boys with the status of apprentices. Later, the establishment of the Royal Military School of Music and, according to H. G. Farmer, the agreement among publishers on a uniform instrumentation in band editions, contributed further to the progress of bands. All the staff bands grew; among the more celebrated bandmasters were Dan Godfrey of the Grenadier Guards (57 players in 1888), Cav. Ladislao Zavertal of the Royal Artillery (91 players near the end of the century), J. A. Kappey of the Chatham Marines and Boosé of the Royal Horse Guards. The Godfreys were a remarkable family; members of several generations of them were distinguished musicians, and many were associated with bands both as conductors and as arrangers.

The need of training bandmasters and of giving bandsmen in the service a sounder musical background impressed James Smyth, then leader of the Royal Artillery Band, and Henry Schallehn, former bandmaster of the Seventeenth Lancers, soon after the middle of the century. Their efforts, backed by influential personages, resulted in the establishment of a Military Music Class at Kneller Hall, near London, in 1857. Kneller Hall became an official institution in 1875, and was given the title of Royal Military School of Music in 1887. After 1875, it was required that all

English bandmasters receive training at that institution, which ever since has been of the greatest influence in maintaining the high standards of English band music.

The development of the band in the United States proceeded along roughly parallel lines. There are records of early bands in Boston and New York, and a number of marches known to have been played at patriotic celebrations in the early days of American independence. The first notable band that has lasted until the present is the United States Marine Band, founded in 1798. Its instrumentation in 1800 was patterned closely on the European models we have described; it consisted of 2 oboes, 2 clarinets, 2 horns, a bassoon and a drum. The band grew gradually. In 1861, its strength was officially authorized as 30 musicians, and in 1899 it was raised to 60. Nearly all the early civilian bands were brass bands. The first mixed wind band of note was the Allentown Band of Allentown, Pennsylvania, founded in 1828.

The founder of the concert band in the United states, and one of the most original and influential bandmasters of all time, was Patrick Sarsfield Gilmore (1829–1892), whose serious accomplishments are sometimes overshadowed by his fame as an organizer of monster festivals. These spectacular affairs, notably those in Boston in 1869 and 1872, made Gilmore's name a vaudeville attraction of the first magnitude. These festivals featured items like the *Fra Diavolo* Overture of Auber, "arranged for orchestra of 1000 performers, 50 trumpeters performing the solo part," or the Anvil Chorus from *Il Trovatore,* with "band of 1000, chorus, etc. . . . 100 members of the Boston Fire Department, playing anvils," or Flotow's *Stradella* Overture, arranged for "reed band of 500 performers." Gilmore was not the first bandmaster to dream up the idea of massing immense numbers of performers, although he seems to have been the first to have hit upon the happy thought of calling in the Fire Department for extra help. Wieprecht had staged a modest affair in 1838, with 1,000 wind players and 200 drummers, the total personnel of 16 infantry and 16 cavalry bands, and even he does not seem to have been the first to take pleasure in this sort of instrumental elephantiasis. Why this type of thing is better than having a football game played with 110 men on each team is not very clear to me, but it appears to be an honored custom which affords much entertainment.

Gilmore was born in Ireland, but came to the United States, via Canada, at an early age, settling in Massachusetts. He was an excellent cornetist, and like many soloists on that instrument, became a bandmaster almost as a matter of course. He led bands in Salem and Boston, and finally organized the band bearing his own name in 1859. During the Civil War, Gilmore and his band served with a Massachusetts regiment. His first immense festival took place in New Orleans in 1864, where he celebrated the inauguration of Governor Hahn with a chorus of 5,000 adults and children, a band of 500, a huge trumpet and drum corps, and lots of artillery. George Upton, in his *Musical Memories,* quotes Gilmore as having told him that "he would be delighted if he could only have church bells, cannons and anvils with every piece he played, not merely for their effect upon audiences, but because he enjoyed them himself."

Despite this taste for noise and fun, Gilmore usually managed to get along on a far more modest scale. It is interesting to note that in 1868 programs advertised "Gilmore's Grand Boston Band" of 25 players. A program given in that year in Providence, Rhode Island, by Gilmore's Band and Orchestra contained selections from *The Bohemian Girl,* the *William Tell* Overture, a medley of popular English tunes and a waltz by Gungl, played by the band. The remaining numbers were played by the orchestra, which also provided the accompaniment for the cornet solo played by the celebrated Matthew Arbuckle.

Gilmore may have wished to outdo the Paris Festival of 1867 in his own festivals at Boston in 1869 and 1872. For the latter, he brought to Boston a number of celebrated foreign and domestic bands, including England's Grenadier Guards, under Daniel Godfrey, Germany's Kaiser Franz Grenadier Regiment, under Heinrich Saro, the Garde Républicaine (founded in that same year, and conducted by Paulus), the National Band of Dublin, led by Edwin Clements, the United States Marine Band, directed by Herman Fries, the 9th Regiment Band of New York, under D. L. Downing, and the Emperor William's Household Cornet Quartette. This event gave the American public, for the first time, an opportunity of hearing some of the best European bands.

After the 1872 festival, Gilmore moved to New York, where he became leader of the band of the 22nd Regiment of New York. He established this band as the finest yet heard in this country, and in 1878 led it in a tour of Europe, where he scored a great critical and popular success. The band had a well-planned instrumentation and compared more than favorably with the best bands anywhere in the world. It was constituted as follows:

2 piccolos
2 flutes
2 oboes
1 A*b* sopranino clarinet
3 E*b* soprano clarinets
16 B*b* clarinets (8, 1st; 4, 2nd; 4, 3rd)
1 alto clarinet
1 bass clarinet
1 soprano saxophone

1 alto saxophone
1 tenor saxophone
1 bass (baritone?) saxophone
2 bassoons
1 contra bassoon
1 E*b* soprano cornet
4 B*b* cornets (1st and 2nd)
2 trumpets
2 fluegelhorns
4 French horns
2 E*b* alto horns
2 B*b* tenor horns
2 euphoniums
3 trombones
5 bombardons (basses)
4 percussion players

Total: 66 players

Gilmore enlarged the size of his band from time to time; in 1892, the last year of his life, he appeared in Madison Square Garden with a band of 83 players, advertised of course as Gilmore's "famous 100-piece band." He had, for all of his eccentricities and stunts, established the concert band in the United States, and had achieved a popularity for himself and his band without any precedent. His successor with the band of the 22nd Regiment was none other than Victor Herbert, who retained the post as bandmaster for six years.

The real successor of Gilmore in popularity and accomplishment was of course John Philip Sousa

(1856–1932), who was appointed leader of the United States Marine Band in 1880, and who resigned that post in 1892 to form his own famous band. Sousa's reputation as both bandmaster and composer of marches was world-wide. He toured Europe five times with his band, and made one trip around the world. It was a European critic who named him "The March King," a title which by popular verdict was justly his. Sousa's first band consisted of 49 players, with the following instrumentation:

2 flutes
2 oboes
2 E*b* clarinets
14 B*b* clarinets
1 alto clarinet
1 bass clarinet
2 bassoons
3 saxophones
4 cornets
2 trumpets
4 French horns
3 trombones
2 euphoniums
4 basses
3 percussion players

Sousa's Band varied in size considerably, reaching a total of 84 players at one time. In his autobiography, *Marching Along,* Sousa gives the following as the instrumentation of his band in 1924, choosing it as representative, and noting the number of instruments used by Gilmore which he had abandoned:

6 flutes (piccolos)
2 oboes
1 English horn
26 B*b* clarinets (14, 1st; 6, 2nd; 6, 3rd)
1 alto clarinet
2 bass clarinets
2 bassoons
4 alto saxophones
2 tenor saxophones
1 baritone saxophone
1 bass saxophone
6 cornets (4, 1st; 2, 2nd)
2 trumpets
4 French horns
4 trombones
2 euphoniums
6 sousaphones (basses)
3 percussion

Total: 75 players

Sousa never staged any gigantic festivals in the Gilmore manner, but like Gilmore he was an excellent showman with a sure understanding of the band's nature as a medium of popular character. His programs featured favorite overtures and concert selections, marches, waltzes and light opera excerpts. Sousa expressed himself quite definitely on the subject of his programs, taking the position that his function was to give the public what it wanted. His success in doing just that was transparently evident, for it is probable that no musical organization in history was known to as many people, or held in greater popular affection, than this great American concert band.

CHAPTER III

The Modern Concert Band

THE READER will have noted how greatly the instrumentation of bands has varied in the course of time, and also to how great a degree the characteristics of bands have varied from country to country. There is today no standard or international instrumentation. The band is still evolving, and it is as impossible today as it was a hundred years ago to define precisely the direction of this evolution. The orchestra, too, is still developing, but its direction is clear: it is, as I have suggested before, the direction composers wish it to take. The orchestra is international because the art of serious musical composition is international. The band, on the other hand, alters its instrumentation as the bandmaster, or a committee of experts, or a military table of organization and equipment sees fit. (In some instances, as with Sax, instrument manufacturers are influential in this respect.) It is still the usage to play any piece of music with whatever musicians the band happens to include. This is true even of the pieces written, and scored, directly for band by important composers.

This situation is due at least in part to the fact

that few bands have been entirely independent artistic organizations. The concert band is an outgrowth of the military band, and in most countries the leading concert bands are still military or semimilitary organizations, following the patterns established in each country for such groups. In the United States, the greatest number of concert bands is found in the highly organized school band movement. Purely civilian and professional bands have never been numerous, and in most countries they are overshadowed by bands of a national or official character. The military band has always functioned as an aspect of national music, and in each country it has been organized along the main lines established by the best known and most influential bandmasters of that country. Thus band instrumentation differs on a national basis, and the differences have in a way become a source of national pride and to some extent even of international rivalry.

Bands in each country, to be sure, play many of the same "classics." One can travel the length and breadth of the world and be sure that each band one encounters will have the *William Tell* Overture in its library. But each band will have a different arrangement of this celebrated war horse, an arrangement perhaps absolutely useless to the band across the nearest border, and possibly even in a different key from any of the others. Moreover, a basic and significant portion of the repertory of bands varies a great deal throughout the world. The marches, for example, are a form of national music, not for export. It is true that the marches of Sousa, Alford, Ganne and many other celebrated composers in this genre have international currency, but at least ninety per cent of all marches written have patriotic or local connotations. An English or American or French band will in all probability play Wagner, but it is unlikely that the march of a Panzer Division will be part of their regular repertory. Martial music is national by nature, and since bands carry on both military and civic traditions they necessarily play a great deal of martial and patriotic music. As media for mass entertainment, they also perform a considerable amount of light music, which as a rule is somewhat less universal than music of symphonic scope. If one examines band programs from various countries, one will find that the band "classics" are the same, but that most of the lighter pieces and original band works are written by the composers of that country. This is true not only of marches and "characteristic" pieces, but even to a large extent of the serious efforts at original band composition. Bandmasters themselves are the most prolific composers of band music, and most of the music they write is by its nature designed for local audiences and tastes. Few bandmasters have been composers of international stature.

These points may appear trivial or even irrelevant, but they are neither. It is not too fanciful to suggest that part of the variation in band instrumentation from country to country is due to the nature of the music played and to the implication of rivalry contained in the semiofficial status of bands. Most nations take great pride in their military bands, and like to feel that their own are the best in such things as size, constitution and smartness. The rivalry is not that of pure music, but one involving many extra-musical factors. From the days of Jean Jacques Rousseau, who deplored the condition of French bands as a national disgrace, people have looked upon bands as symbols of national prestige. Nearly all efforts to improve or enlarge the instrumentation of bands have been made not on a basis of better music as an international art, but on one of national reform and accomplishment.

There have been discussions from time to time about the advantages of establishing a standard international instrumentation for wind bands. Until there is an international band literature of really serious proportions, and until bandmasters are prepared and able to play it in exact accordance with the composer's score, it is doubtful that these discussions will lead to any action. It is furthermore to be doubted that any great gain would be involved, except perhaps to publishers of music. The establishment, on some necessarily arbitrary basis, of a standard instrumentation, not only puts the cart before the horse but would in all probability result in artistic ossification rather than expansion. Ideally, music is international (we have all heard it described as a universal language), but realistically it can be, as much band music is, as extremely and peculiarly national as language or flags or regional menus or a sense of humor. The characteristic bands today are those of armies and of schools; it is a fair guess that bands will become international in practice about as soon as will the institutions of which they are adjuncts.

For the time being, at any rate, we must deal with bands not only generally, but with attention to their specific differences. For practical reasons, therefore, our detailed study of bands will be limited to those of the United States, where, as we shall observe, differences exist according to type and purpose within the framework of a general similarity. No study would, however, be complete without comparative data on bands in other parts of the world, and in order that an idea may be formed of typical instrumentations, a few notes follow.

A representative English band is that maintained at the Royal Military School of Music (Kneller Hall), where bandmasters for the British military receive their training. This school not only provides a curriculum which assures competent musicianship on the part of its graduates, but is a great factor in maintaining the traditions and high standards of British band music. In recent years, the band at Kneller Hall consisted of the following instruments:

piccolo
flutes
E*b* clarinets (1st and 2nd)
oboes (1st and 2nd)
B*b* clarinets (solo, 1st, 2nd and 3rd)
E*b* alto saxophone
B*b* tenor saxophone
bassoons (1st and 2nd)
4 horns in F
cornets (1st and 2nd)
trumpets (1st and 2nd)
3 trombones
euphonium
basses (E*b* and BB*b*)
percussion

One of the most famous bands in the world is that of the Garde Républicaine of Paris. This band was formed in 1872, as a result of the merger of the two leading bands of the French capital. It has had a distinguished succession of conductors, including Sellenick, Paulus, Parès, Balay and Dupont, many of whom have been active as composers and arrangers for bands. Its instrumentation in recent years is indicated by the scoring of Florent Schmitt's *Dionysiaques,* written for this band in 1925:

2 piccolos, C
2 or 4 flutes, C
2 oboes
1 or 2 English horns
2 or 4 bassoons
1 or 2 contrabass sarrusophones, C

2 or 4 E*b* clarinets
26 B*b* clarinets
2 or 4 bass clarinets
1 or 2 contrabass clarinets

2 or 4 alto saxophones
2 or 4 tenor saxophones
2 or 4 baritone saxophones
1 or 2 bass saxophones

2 or 4 trumpets in C
2 or 4 cornets in B*b*
2 or 4 horns in F
1st and 2nd trombones (tenor)
3rd trombone (bass in C)

1 soprano saxhorn (fluegelhorn)
4 or 8 B*b* fluegelhorns
3 E*b* altos
2 baritones, B*b*
6 basses, B*b*
6 contrabasses, BB*b*
2 or 4 string basses

percussion, including celesta, xylophone, 3 timpani and usual effects.

(Many of the parts are marked *ad libitum*).

Bands in Italy are typified by Rome's Banda Municipale, whose most famous leader was Alessandro Vessella, a composer and arranger of note, and the author of a textbook on band arranging which is used in many Latin countries. The Banda Municipale of Rome, following Vessella's pattern, has the following instrumentation:

1 piccolo in D*b*
2 flutes in C
1 sopranino clarinet in A*b*
1 soprano clarinet in E*b*
1st, 2nd and 3rd B*b* clarinets

2 alto clarinets
2 bass clarinets
4 saxophones (soprano, alto, tenor, baritone)
1 soprano fluegelhorn in E*b*
2 B*b* fluegelhorns
2 B*b* cornets
2 B*b* trumpets
2 E*b* trumpets
4 French horns
2 altos in E*b*
2 tenor horns in B*b*
1 baritone
1 euphonium
2 tenor trombones
1 bass trombone
1 contrabass trombone
basses in E*b* and BB*b*
percussion

Russian "horn bands" were famous in the eighteenth and nineteenth centuries as one of the world's greatest musical curiosities. These bands varied from 37 to 60 players, each of whom performed on a horn capable of sounding *only one note!* Although the subject is not particularly pertinent to contemporary Russian bands, I feel that there may be both interest and amusement in the following description of these bands, abridged from J. A. Kappey's *A Short History of Military Music*:

"Such a band can only be compared to an organ, each pipe of which was sounded by a human being. In the political state of Russia at that time, the serfs were utilized like any other 'raw material', and it was not considered a waste of labour, if the result contributed to the entertainment of the 'proprietors'. The first band consisted of 37 musicians, each having a horn the tonic of which formed a note of the chromatic scale of three octaves. The first performance . . . took place in 1751, and met with immense success. The novelty lay in the fact that for the first time a brass-band departed from the fossilized pattern of trumpet music, with its wearisome limitation to three chords, and modulated easily through any harmonic progression.

"The instruments being made as perfectly in tune as possible, and the sounding of the notes being studied with great care and labour, it is said that the performances of that band, with regard to shading and purity of intonation, were of the most perfect kind ever heard. The number of horns and performers was at last increased to 60, and their training was so careful that they performed pieces of the best classical composers of the time; nay, the 'almost impossible' was achieved, when in 1775 the opera 'Alceste' by Raupach was performed complete, recitatives and all, by a band of this description. . . . The notation of the parts was simple, the main point of it being the time. . . . During the enormously numerous rehearsals of a piece . . . [such as] some fugue by Bach, the time was given by the sound of a bell, and bar after bar had to be mechanically drilled, until at last the whole organism performed with the regularity of a musical box. As a curiosity Russian horn music deserves mention, especially as many years ago one of their bands made a concert tour through Europe, and created quite a furore by its wonderful performance. As an example of the waste of human labour it stands unique; as a practical extension of the resources of art it is useless and quite laid aside."

Bands on the European pattern appeared in Russia at an early date. There is every evidence that band music is extremely popular in Russia today, and that military music is highly regarded. A recent band score from Russia calls for the following instruments:

piccolo
flute
oboe (ad lib)
B*b* clarinets (1st, 2nd and 3rd)
bassoons (ad lib)
1st and 2nd cornets
1st and 2nd trumpets
1st and 2nd E*b* altos
4 horns in E*b* (3rd and 4th horns ad lib)
3 tenor horns in B*b*
B*b* baritone
basses
percussion (no timpani)

A later score from Russia has approximately the same instrumentation except for the addition of an

E*b* clarinet. This instrumentation is interestingly small compared to that common in the United States and most other countries.

Spanish bands in the nineteenth century enjoyed some celebrity as having the fanciest instrumentation, as to both size and constitution, of any bands in Europe. I am indebted to Mr. Pedro Sanjuan, distinguished composer and founder of the Havana Philharmonic Orchestra, who was also for some years a bandmaster in Madrid, for the following information on the composition of a modern Spanish wind band:

piccolo
1st and 2nd flutes
1st and 2nd oboes
E*b* clarinet
B*b* clarinets (solo, 1st, 2nd, 3rd)
alto clarinet (large bands only)
bass clarinet (large bands only)
1st and 2nd bassoons (large bands only)
5 saxophones (soprano, alto, tenor, baritone, bass)
1st and 2nd cornets
1st and 2nd trumpets
2 B*b* fluegelhorns (used as solo instruments)
4 French horns (replaced by E*b* altos in small bands)
2 E*b* altos (used *with* horns in large bands)
2 baritones
small tuba in B*b* (euphonium)
tubas in E*b* or F, and in BB*b*
violoncellos and string basses (in large bands)
percussion (timpani in large bands only)

South America has many bands of impressive size and quality. The instrumentation is generally patterned after that favored by Vessella. Typical of South American bands is the excellent Banda Nacional of Bogotá, Colombia, directed by José Rozo Contreras, a pupil of Vessella. The instrumentation is as follows:

1 piccolo in C
2 flutes
2 oboes
1 English horn
1 soprano clarinet in A*b*
2 soprano clarinets in E*b*
20 B*b* clarinets (10, 1st; 10, 2nd)
2 alto clarinets
2 bass clarinets
6 saxophones (soprano, 2 altos, tenor, baritone and bass)
2 bassoons
1 contrabass sarrusophone in E*b*
1 soprano fluegelhorn in E*b*
4 fluegelhorns in B*b*
2 cornets in B*b*
2 trumpets in E*b*
2 trumpets in B*b* (low)
4 horns in F
2 alto horns in E*b*
2 tenor horns in B*b*
2 tenor trombones
1 bass trombone in F
2 euphoniums
4 tubas in F, E*b* and BB*b*

4 string basses
percussion (including timpani, chimes, carillon, celesta, drums, etc.)

One of the finest concert bands in the world is the Philippine Army Band (formerly known as the Philippine Constabulary Band), an organization of 100 players. Its large instrumentation is based purely on Western models, no native or exotic instruments being employed.

The reader may be interested in the fact that wind bands in the Western style are very popular in Japan, and that the excellence of Japanese bands is attested by musicians who have heard them perform. As early as 1890, a French musician traveling in the Orient, was struck by the incongruity of hearing a performance of excerpts from Verdi's *La Traviata* given by a band of Japanese in Tokyo. Lieutenant Colonel Howard C. Bronson and Dr. Edwin Franko Goldman, visiting Tokyo in 1945, were impressed by the playing of the Tokyo Metropolitan Band, which, they state, is similar to American bands in instrumentation except that tenor horns in B*b* are used, as well as both French horns and E*b* altos. Japanese wind bands represent an exception in so far as the national patterning of bands is concerned. The Japanese wind band is a pure and simple imitation of Western musical usage, and has of course no connection whatsoever with the indigenous music of the country. It is said that many Japanese have written compositions for band, and that these too are patterned closely after Western music.

Bands in the United States may be grouped in three main classes: the professional civilian band, the military band, and the school or college band. While all these are "concert" bands, within the broad definition of that term, each type has different functions and problems, organizationally and artistically. To arrive at a clear idea of the nature of the concert band today, it is necessary that these problems and functions be studied and compared.

The first important concert band in the United States, composed of professional civilian musicians, and not connected with a military or municipal institution, was the one organized by Gilmore. That celebrated bandmaster flourished at a time when there were few good bands or symphony orchestras in the country, and when a professional concert band could be made a paying proposition. The professional band has always had to compete with bands supported at public expense, and its nature has always been in part determined by the simple facts that the musicians must be paid and that the bandmaster or impresario likes to remain solvent. The instrumentation of the professional civilian band has often been influenced by these purely practical considerations.

Gilmore's Band varied in size according to the dictates of business as well as of art. Although he liked a large band, and appeared when he could with a band of 100, he generally used fewer men and often performed with no more than 25 players. Sousa, too, usually toured with a smaller band than he would have liked or than he maintained during a steady engagement in one place.

When not operating under its own auspices, the professional band is often hired to perform by managers who specify a certain number of players. Instead of engaging a band with its full complement, it is customary to request a band "of 30 men," or whatever number the budget allows. Most conscientious professional bandmasters of course refuse to perform with fewer men than the minimum they feel necessary for artistic performance. It has, however, often been necessary to modify the constitution of a band for commercial reasons.

In the heyday of Gilmore and Sousa, competition from radio and recording was nonexistent, the public taste for the symphony orchestra was less developed, and fewer large bands were supported by public funds. The concert band also occupied something of the position today enjoyed by the popular dance orchestras. Marches, polkas and waltzes, played by bands, were the vogue for dancing before a new type of dance orchestra or jazz band came along with the fox trot and the tango. Bandmasters of that period therefore benefited by being able to combine concert music with a type of popular music then in the height of fashion. In popular estimation they occupied positions analogous to those of today's swing idols.

Very few bands of this independent type can now manage to remain active on a large scale. Except for special circumstances, band concerts have generally been free concerts, given either by military bands maintained by the armed services or by municipal park bands paid by cities and towns. In the United States, as in Europe, free band concerts in public places are traditional. When private professional bands give such concerts, it is evident that funds must be provided in some way. The difficulty of reconciling free concerts and paid musicians has been one of the principal reasons for the scarcity of "proprietary," or privately supported, professional concert bands.

The type of professional band maintained by Gilmore and Sousa is today best represented in the United States by the Goldman Band. This band was organized in 1911 by Edwin Franko Goldman, whose aim was to perform the finest type of music with the same artistic sincerity and excellence as characterized the symphony orchestras of which he had been a member. The personnel of the band was chosen from the best professional musicians available in New York. In 1918, the Goldman Band began giving regular seasons of free outdoor concerts in New York under private auspices. The concerts were given at Columbia University, and the necessary money was raised by subscription through the personal efforts of the bandmaster. After the success of these concerts on that basis had been assured and recognized for many years, the support of the concerts was undertaken by the Guggenheim family and the concerts were removed, at the request of New York City, to the Mall in New York's Central Park. They have never been municipal concerts, however, as the band remains a private organization receiving no public funds.

The instrumentation of the Goldman Band (1946) is as follows:

1 piccolo
3 flutes (all doubling on piccolo)
2 oboes (2nd doubling on English horn)
1 E*b* clarinet
19 B*b* clarinets (1st, 2nd, 3rd)
1 bass clarinet
2 bassoons
1 alto saxophone
1 tenor saxophone
1 baritone saxophone
4 cornets
3 trumpets
4 horns in F
6 trombones (4 tenor, 2 bass)
2 euphoniums
4 tubas

1 string bass
1 harp
3 percussion
Total: 60 players

The instrumentation and numerical strength of the Goldman Band has remained fairly constant since its foundation. The alto clarinet, once used in the band, was discarded by Dr. Goldman as being of doubtful value in the ensemble. Like Sousa, Dr. Goldman for many years did not use an E*b* clarinet, not because of the instrument's lack of value, but because no player of the requisite ability was available.

A professional band of this type has of course no functions of a military nature, nor is it affected by any of the organizational or other nonmusical considerations which concern military, municipal or amateur bands. It exists only to give concerts, the caliber of which is the artistic responsibility of the conductor. Its repertory must be large and varied, especially in the case of a band like the Goldman Band, which gives sixty concerts on successive nights each summer without repeating a single program. As the leading example of this type of band in the United States, the Goldman Band, under Dr. Goldman's direction, has exerted a considerable influence on band music throughout the nation. It has, as a matter of artistic principle and because of the nature of its audiences, been extremely receptive to new band music, both arrangements and original compositions, and has done much to enlarge the scope of the band's repertory. Many of these arrangements and original works have been written at Dr. Goldman's request for performance at his concerts.

Municipal bands are the direct descendants of the town bands discussed in the preceding chapter. In the nineteenth century, there were many town and city bands throughout the United States, but there are today perhaps fewer than at any previous time, and most of these are relatively small in size and constituted on a part-time basis. Permanent bands in the larger cities receive as a rule inadequate financial support, while in smaller towns their functions have been taken over to some extent by the high school bands. Many cities offer a few concerts in the parks during the summer months, but these are generally given by temporary bands assembled for the occasion. Permanent municipal bands still active today are, it is interesting to note, principally in smaller cities such as Hagerstown, Maryland, Allentown, Pennsylvania, and Fort Dodge, Iowa, although San Francisco and a few other large cities continue to support bands.

The band maintained by a business or industrial concern represents another type of professional civilian band. Such bands are also apparently fewer in number today than some years ago, and it is only just to observe that they were never as common in the

United States as in England. Many of these bands were and are composed of amateurs with a sprinkling of professional players to lend strength, but others have been made up of professional musicians hired as such, and as a rule performing other work for the company. Some of these bands, which exist partly for the recreation of the employees and partly as an advertisement for the firm, have been thoroughly professional in the quality of their performances, notably the Armco Band of Cincinnati, directed by Frank Simon, and the band of the Arma Company of Brooklyn, directed by Erik W. G. Leidzén. Such bands as these have been true concert bands with complete instrumentation and a high caliber of musicianship.

Military bands in the United States are of various types. The organization, size and character of these bands are, of course, determined by official legislation and regulation, so that they differ in many important respects from civilian bands. The regimental and divisional bands of the United States army have as a rule been small; regimental bands have by regulation consisted of as few as 16 men, although for a brief period as many as 48 were authorized. According to most critics, American line bands have been inadequate, and suffer in comparison with similar bands in other countries. True concert bands in the armed services are, with three exceptions, of fairly recent establishment. The United States Marine Band, as has been noted, was founded in 1798; the bands of the United States Military and Naval Academies date from the first part of the nineteenth century. The United States Army Band and the United States Navy Band were organized after the close of World War I, while the Army Air Forces Band took shape at the beginning of World War II. These bands now are the major permanent bands of concert type belonging to the United States military and naval establishment, and they compare favorably with any bands in the world. All of them are large in size, with full instrumentation and professional players, and all are conducted by commissioned officers.

Typical of these concert bands in the armed services is that of the Army Air Forces. This band, directed by Captain George S. Howard, is the newest of the large service bands, and has the following instrumentation since its reorganization after the termination of World War II:

6 flutes (all doubling on piccolo)
3 oboes (one doubling on English horn)
1 E*b* clarinet
14 B*b* clarinets
1 alto clarinet
1 bass clarinet
5 saxophones (2 alto, 2 tenor, 1 baritone)
4 bassoons (one doubling on contra bassoon, and one on bass sarrusophone)

11 cornets and trumpets
8 horns in F
6 trombones (4 tenor, 2 bass)
3 baritones
4 tubas
4 violoncellos
4 string basses
6 percussion
Total: 81 players

Considerations of space prevent listing the instrumentation of the other major service bands: the Navy Band, directed by Lieutenant Charles Brendler, the Marine Band, under Captain William F. Santelmann, the Army Band, conducted by Captain Thomas F. Darcy, Jr., the Band of the United States Military Academy (West Point), directed by Captain Francis E. Resta, and the Band of the United States Naval Academy, under Lieutenant William R. Sima. All are large bands, musical organizations of great versatility, which give equally excellent performances of serious concert music and works of a patriotic or martial character. In addition to giving regular concerts, these bands provide music for many official ceremonies in Washington and elsewhere. Nearly all of them perform as orchestras as well, by the addition of violins and violas and the subtraction of some wind instruments, following the pattern set by the English Royal Artillery Band. The service bands also divide into smaller units, such as dance orchestras, to provide music for entertainments and special occasions.

Authorized divisional bands in the army were, during World War II, composed of 56 players. Few of these bands were maintained at full strength, however. The authorized instrumentation was:

3 flutes or piccolos
1 oboe
1 E*b* clarinet
12 B*b* clarinets
1 alto clarinet
1 bass clarinet
1 bassoon
3 alto saxophones
3 tenor saxophones
1 baritone saxophone
6 cornets
4 trumpets
4 horns in F
2 baritones
6 trombones
5 tubas
2 drums

Divisional bands of full strength, with the instrumentation authorized, function very adequately as concert bands, although they have military duties of greater importance than the giving of concerts. Aside from marching and ceremonies, their mission of upholding morale necessitates providing music for entertainments and dances. Functionally, these bands are really agglomerations of smaller units, which are of more practical use than a large concert band and are in greater demand among the troops.

All other bands of the Army Ground Forces, Army Service Forces and Army Air Forces have an authorized strength of 28 players. These small bands are designed primarily as marching and recreational bands, and are not concert bands in the sense we have been discussing. The authorized instrumentation is:

1 flute or piccolo
1 E*b* clarinet
6 B*b* clarinets
3 saxophones
4 cornets
2 trumpets
3 horns
1 baritone
3 trombones
2 tubas
2 drums

The Navy, too, maintains bands on capital ships and at various shore installations. These bands are generally small, averaging perhaps 16 men, and do duty partly as maritime equivalents of regimental bands and partly as dance combinations. A Navy School of Music for the training of these musicians is maintained in Washington under the direction of Lieutenant J. Thurmond.

Bands of a semimilitary character are maintained

by the police and fire departments of some large cities. These are usually composed of professional and amateur musicians, directed by a professional musician holding an honorary position in the department. These bands function at official parades and ceremonies, and at departmental affairs, and in general characteristics resemble the army bands from which they derive. Many American Legion posts and Masonic or fraternal orders also maintain bands of a semimilitary character, these too being often composed of mixed amateur and professional personnel and performing chiefly at patriotic celebrations, parades or organizational affairs. They do not, as a rule, function as concert bands.

Bands in American colleges and universities have come a long way from the days of the small nondescript groups which once assaulted the ears at football games. Today these bands are highly developed, well instrumented, regularly rehearsed, and usually directed by full-time bandmasters. Band music is taken very seriously as a part of the music program in many institutions, which give full academic credit for band work. The players are, of course, amateurs and students; yet there seems to be little difficulty in finding or training players on the rarer wind instruments, especially since most of the players receive their first band training in high school and are no

The Band of H. M. Grenadier Guards, London, England. Dan Godfrey, Bandmaster. This photograph was taken at Boston, Mass., in 1872. The band was taking part in the International Peace Jubilee held there that summer and was received with great enthusiasm. It was the first time a British soldier had appeared in uniform in the United States since the War of Independence.

A Brass Band of Fiji Islanders. The instrumentation follows the conventional pattern, except for the presence of the solitary B*b* clarinet. The uniforms are unconventional.
From the collection of Edwin Franko Goldman, Mt. Tremper, N. Y.

longer beginners when they reach college. Interest in band music is such that many of the university bands are extremely large and will admit only really competent players. The performances achieved by many of them are often on the highest possible level of technical excellence.

A model of university band organization is provided by the bands of the University of Michigan, directed by William D. Revelli, one of the new generation of musicianly bandmasters and a recognized leader in his field. Michigan bands are composed of three units: the Marching Band, the Varsity Band and the Concert Band. These bands have a combined membership of between 175 and 200 students, both men and women except in the Marching Band, for which men only are eligible. Audition is a prerequisite to membership, and only players of suitable proficiency may become members of any band. (This is rather a different story from the fairly recent days when the author attended college, when anyone who even owned or could borrow an instrument was welcomed into the band with delight!)

The Marching Band at the University of Michigan is made up of members of the Varsity and Concert Bands, and consists of 128 players. Its activities are confined to the fall athletic season, at the close of which its members return to the Varsity or Concert Band. It should be noted parenthetically that the

Marching Band has reached a degree of virtuosity in some midwestern universities which probably surpasses anything ever before seen. The formations and maneuvers, all executed while the bands are playing (and generally playing well), can be described only by the Hollywood term "colossal." We have already remarked upon the continuance of the military band tradition as carried on in these marching bands, but the schools and universities have provided some elaborate refinements on the old parade-ground formations.

Instruments such as bassoons, English horns, alto and bass clarinets, oboes and flutes are not used in the University of Michigan Marching Band. They are of course included in the Concert Band, which normally numbers about 100 players, distributed as follows:

8 to 10 flutes
3 to 4 oboes (English horn)
24 to 28 B*b* clarinets
3 alto clarinets
3 bass clarinets
3 to 4 bassoons
5 to 6 saxophones (alto, tenor and baritone)
6 to 8 cornets
2 trumpets
6 to 8 French horns
4 baritones or euphoniums
6 trombones
6 tubas
2 string basses

1 or 2 harps
4 to 6 percussion

An E*b* clarinet and 2 fluegelhorns are occasionally added.

The players in the concert band devote an average of not less than ten hours a week to band work throughout the school year. The concert band has three regular rehearsals per week, totaling four and one-half hours, with sectional rehearsals held intermittently and special rehearsals when necessary. Several formal concerts are given each year, and music is provided for many campus activities. Music for basketball games and similar events is provided by the Varsity Band, joined by various players from the Concert Band.

The organization of band work at the University of Michigan is a model of efficiency, and shows clearly how much thought and time are given to band music there and at other large universities where similar systems are in use. Mr. Revelli is assisted by a student conductor, a student manager, a chief librarian and staff, and an equipment manager. The assistant dean of students functions as faculty business manager. A Band Constitution regulates all matters of organization and procedure, and a small printed card containing band rules and regulations is given each member. There are printed application blanks for band candidates and standard forms for audition records. All music in the library is neatly catalogued on special cards of several colors. Uniforms are owned by the university and issued to band members upon payment of a small deposit. The university also owns a number of instruments, which are issued to selected students upon order of the director of bands. It can thus be seen that the university band is an enterprise of considerable magnitude, which, although deriving historically from the military band and assuming in many respects the function of the professional concert band, is something comparatively new and of the highest importance in the development of band music.

High school band music, like that in the colleges and universities, is a peculiarly American phenomenon. Instruction in instrumental music began on a small scale early in the century, but by the 1920's it had become widespread and highly organized. There are today in the United States uncountable thousands of high school bands, whose activities are integrated by the National High School Band Association. In some high schools it would appear that band music receives as much attention as the teaching of English, history or mathematics. Annual festivals and contests, on local, regional and national scales, are a feature of the high school music scene. The problems of the high school bandmaster are, of course, largely those of teaching. The players as a rule must receive instruction on their instruments at the same time as they are being trained as part of a band. The high school band is therefore a teaching and rehearsing organization, rather than a purely concert-giving group. Each concert given by one of these bands requires many times its length in hours of preparation; hence formal concerts, aside from the usual "campus" activities, are seldom more than a few each school year. However, the concerts given by some high school bands are on an extraordinarily high level, and it is as concert bands that these groups must be considered.

The National High School Band Association has established recommended instrumentations for school bands of Classes A, B and C (classification depending on the size of the school, not the proficiency of the players). As these are important, in that they show a pattern for instrumentation which is regarded as "ideal" or highly desirable, they are reproduced in full, as given in the School Music Competition-Festivals Manual for 1943:

(HIGH SCHOOLS)

INSTRUMENTATION

Standard Instrumentation for Symphonic Band

(Suggested for Class A Schools)

5 flutes (one or two interchangeable with piccolo)
2 E*b* clarinets (2 E*b* clarinets may be replaced by 2 addi-

tional C or E*b* flutes, or 1 E*b* clarinet and 1 or more C or E*b* flutes)
24 or more B*b* clarinets
2 alto clarinets
2 bass clarinets
2 or more oboes (one doubling English horn when called for in score)
2 or more bassoons
5 saxophones (soprano, alto [or two altos], tenor, baritone, and bass. Large bands may double this number.)
4 or more B*b* cornets
2 or more B*b* trumpets
2 fluegelhorns
4 to 8 French horns
4 to 6 trombones
2 to 4 baritones
2 E*b* tubas
4 BB*b* tubas
2 string basses
1 harp (if available and called for in score)
1 timpani
3 other percussion

Total 75 or more players

Suggested Instrumentation for Class B Bands

5 flutes (1 or 2 interchangeable with piccolo)
1 E*b* clarinet (may be replaced by an E*b* flute or an additional C flute)
24 B*b* clarinets
2 alto clarinets
2 bass clarinets
2 oboes
2 bassoons

6 saxophones (must include two altos, one tenor, and one baritone)
4 cornets
4 trumpets
2 fluegelhorns
} may substitute two trumpets for two additional cornets, but not more than ten to be used in this group
6 French horns
4 baritones
6 trombones
2 E*b* tubas
4 BB*b* tubas (string bass may be used as a substitute)
1 timpani
3 other percussion
harp (if available and called for in the score may be substituted for any of the above)

Total 80 or more players

Suggested Instrumentation for Class C Bands

4 flutes (interchangeable with piccolo as needed)
1 E*b* clarinet (may be replaced by an E*b* flute or an additional C flute)
18 to 20 B*b* clarinets
2 alto clarinets
2 bass clarinets
2 oboes
2 bassoons
4 to 6 saxophones
6 cornets
2 trumpets
2 fluegelhorns (two additional trumpets may be used as substitutes)
6 French horns
3 baritones — Not more than thirteen in this group.
4 trombones

2 E*b* tubas
4 BB*b* tubas (one string bass may be used as a substitute)
1 timpani
3 other percussion

Total 68 or more players

It is of course impossible for each high school to conform exactly to these schemes of instrumentation. Nevertheless, it is remarkable that most high school bands manage to maintain fairly elaborate instrumentations, with players on oboe and bassoon as well as on the ever-popular cornet and saxophone. Many high schools have junior and senior bands, promoting players from the former to the latter when they have advanced sufficiently. As an example of the actual instrumentation of a good high school band which has done well in many contests, that of the Lenoir (North Carolina) High School may be cited. This band, directed by Captain James C. Harper, consisted of 85 players in 1946, with the following instrumentation:

6 flutes in C
2 flutes in E*b*
2 oboes
24 B*b* clarinets (4, solo; 5, 1st; 9, 2nd; 6, 3rd)
2 alto clarinets
3 bass clarinets
3 bassoons
4 alto saxophones
1 tenor saxophone

1 baritone saxophone
12 cornets or trumpets (4 each on 1st, 2nd and 3rd parts)
7 horns
4 baritones
4 trombones
4 tubas
6 percussion

Harp and string bass are included when available, and the band sometimes numbers as many as 92 players.

High school bands are the typical bands of America today. Professional musicians, and the problems of professional serious music, have no place in this world, which is a special one. The organization and equipment of many high school bands are comparable in kind to those found in the larger universities, although in most cases the activity is on a smaller scale. The interest of the high school music movement is in music education rather than in music in the abstract, and its aims and accomplishments must be viewed in that light. The influence which the high school band movement exerts on band music in general cannot be minimized. It may safely be said that little band music is published in the United States which is not in line, both technically and musically, with the needs or policies of the school organizations. It is almost inevitable that the direction taken by the high school bands will determine the direction for better or worse of band music as a whole in America.

Although brass bands are not concert bands of the type we have been discussing, they should be mentioned here if only because so many people still refer to *all* military or concert bands as "brass bands." The brass band is the modern descendant of the cavalry band, which traditionally was composed only of trumpets and horns and drums. Wieprecht's reform of the cavalry bands of the Prussian army, to which reference has been made, was the impetus for a great popular movement toward the formation of civilian bands constructed on the cavalry model. The universal adoption of valves, and the convincing demonstration of their usefulness given by Wieprecht, extended the musical possibilities of brass instruments so obviously that immense enthusiasm was manifested for exploring the effect of various brass combinations. The first popular brass bands in England were organized in about 1833, and their number soon multiplied. Until Gilmore's day, most of the bands in the United States were brass bands. The American Brass Band, active in New England in the 1850's under the leadership of W. F. Marshall, was composed of the following instruments:

E*b* bugle
E*b* cornet

B*b* bugle
posthorn
trumpet
2 alto horns
2 tenor horns
baritone
3 basses
side drum, bass drum, cymbals

This was a representative brass band of those times. Brass bands have declined in popularity in the United States, but they are still the characteristic popular amateur bands in England, occupying there a position roughly comparable to that of the high school band in America. It is said that brass bands were encouraged originally in England in order to provide wholesome relaxation for factory and mine workers. These bands are still for the most part associated with industrial enterprises and collieries. Brass band festivals and contests are regular events.

The music which brass bands can play is astonishingly varied, although the limitations of the instruments are apparent. At one time it was common practice to add one E*b* clarinet to the instrumentation of the brass band, in order to add a higher voice than that provided by the E*b* cornet, or fluegelhorn. (The reader will note a solitary clarinet, probably in B*b*, in the Fijian Brass Band pictured in this volume.) In England, a brass band repertory of considerable size has been developed, and original compositions for brass band have been written by a number of leading composers, including Elgar, John Ireland, Gustav Holst, Granville Bantock and Herbert Howells. There are also a number of interesting works written for brass band by some of France's most famous composers.

Typical instrumentation of a modern brass band is as follows:

E*b* soprano cornet
solo, 1st and 2nd B*b* cornets
fluegelhorn in B*b*
3 E*b* altos
2 B*b* baritones or tenor horns
3 trombones
euphonium
2 tubas
drums

The standard English brass band is composed of 24 players.

The examples given in this chapter should give the reader an idea of the types and organizations of bands in the United States and abroad. The most important categories have been mentioned, and it should be obvious that the problems and functions of bands differ so widely that one cannot speak of "*the* concert band" as simply as one can discuss "*the* symphony orchestra." Standard instrumentations for all American concert bands have been suggested many times, notably by the American Bandmasters Association, a group which includes leading professional, military and school bandmasters. That no standard has been adopted is not due to willful resistance on anyone's part, but rather to the differing circumstances under which bands and bandmasters of necessity operate, as well as to the lack of an international band repertory of serious dimensions. Even such a repertory, however, would not bridge the gap between the professional and the amateur band, since their approaches to it would necessarily be different.

All these bands have something in common: they are manifestations of a popular musical culture which finds in them an expression of something not provided by any other type of concert organization. Most important, they are a form of local, or regional, or national organization fulfilling a genuine community need and serving a genuine community interest. Whatever their instrumentations, and whatever their special circumstances, they serve the useful purpose of bringing many people into firsthand contact with live music.

CHAPTER IV

The Instrumentation of the Modern Band

HAVING NOTED the instrumentations of various bands, past and present, we may now proceed to an examination of band instrumentation in general, and to a discussion of how the instruments of the band are used. Bands today are composed of some combination of the following instruments:

Flutes

piccolo in C
piccolo in D*b*
flutes in C, D*b* or E*b*
fifes in B*b*

Double Reeds

oboe
English horn
heckelphone
bass oboe
bassoon
contra bassoon
sarrusophones:
 sopranino in E*b* to contrabass in E*b*

Single Reeds

Clarinets:
 sopranino in A*b*
 soprano in E*b*
 clarinet in B*b*
 alto in E*b*
 bass in B*b*
 contrabass in E*b* or **BB*b***
Saxophones:
 soprano in B*b*
 alto in E*b*
 tenor in B*b*
 baritone in E*b*
 bass in B*b*

Strings

violoncello
string bass
harp

Brasses

trumpet in E*b* (high)
trumpet in B*b*
trumpet in E*b* (low)
trombone in B*b* (tenor)
trombone in B*b*, G, F or E*b* (bass)
cornet in E*b* (high)
cornet in B*b*
French horn in F or B*b*
Saxhorns:
 fluegelhorn in E*b* (high)
 fluegelhorn in B*b*
 alto horn in E*b*
 mellophone
 tenor horn in B*b*
 baritone in B*b*
 euphonium in B*b*
 tubas in B*b*, C, F, E*b* and BB*b*.

Percussion

timpani
bass drum
snare drum
cymbals
chimes
xylophone
triangle
tambourine
wood block
celesta
gongs
castanets, etc.

Many of these instruments are used infrequently or not at all in the orchestra. Others, which are found in the orchestra, are used so differently in the band that they assume another character. We shall discuss first the ensemble of the band, as a medium for the performance of music, and in the following chapter take up the separate instruments and the problems they present.

The outstanding fact about the wind instruments used in bands is that nearly all of them are built in flat keys, mostly B*b* and E*b*. There were originally a number of sound acoustical reasons for constructing the brass instruments in this manner, but by and large the general adoption of flat keys is a matter of tradition. What construction in flat keys means is simply that the fundamental tones of the brass instruments will be the tonics of flat keys like B*b* or E*b*, and that the open tones, or harmonics of the fundamental, will be the series starting from that note, the fifth, the octave, and so on. While modern instruments, no matter what their pitch, are capable of playing all notes of a chromatic scale, the valve or key fingering is easier in the natural scale of the instrument. In orchestral music, this idiosyncrasy of the wind instruments was formerly met by specifying instruments in appropriate keys (horns in D, trumpets in G, clarinets in A, and so forth); in modern orchestral writing, the practice is to shift the responsibility to the player. Parts are generally written for horn in F, trumpet in B*b* and clarinet in B*b*, since orchestral players on these instruments are accustomed to using them for music in any key.

In bands, however, by reason of the preponderance of B*b* and E*b* instruments, nearly all music is written in flat keys. Theoretically the band sounds best when playing in a flat key because more of the open tones of the brasses may be used, and it is still maintained by some musicians that these tones have a greater purity than the tones produced with the use of valves. That argument, with modern instruments, is of doubtful validity. The important argument is that the fingering of the instruments is easier in flat keys. That is the determining consideration in the choice of keys for band music.

As constituted today, the band tends to be out of balance; it often produces a sound of which the outstanding characteristic is its thickness. Most of the instruments found in quantity in a band have thick or heavy sounds: the saxhorns, clarinets and saxophones, for example. These instruments are also largely grouped in the middle registers, giving the band an overweight which is made even more apparent by its weakness in the extreme top register. The additions made to the instrumentation of the modern band have mostly been instruments of middle and low register, while the higher instruments have been disappearing. There is nothing in the band even remotely comparable to the top tones of the violins, nor does the flute stand out against the heavy blend of clarinets and cornets with the clarity it possesses in the orchestra. The high registers of the clarinets are shrill, unpleasant, and usually out of tune.

The lowest register of the band suffers from a different handicap: not a lack of instruments, but a too great variety. The tuba is a useful and satisfactory instrument, capable, in the hands of an expert, of performing almost any bass part. It is nevertheless a slow-speaking and thick-sounding affair, and few players make it sound more musical than a foghorn. As it is usually played, it is certainly a far from satisfactory substitute for a string bass, which, aside from greater agility, also gives the impression of greater clarity with respect to pitch. The tuba is, however, the primary bass instrument of the band; it is reinforced by other instruments, which, whatever their individual virtues, add up to a peculiar and not always pleasant effect. The bassoon, which speaks and sounds better than any other low wind instrument is, unfortunately, not an important member of the wind band. It is outweighed and outnumbered, and in small bands is often conspicuous by its complete absence. In his campaign against the bassoon, Sax did the band a huge disservice. The combination of tubas, bass saxophones, bassoons, contrabass sarrusophones, euphoniums and bass clarinets is, in any case, one of the least satisfactory parts of the band. I refrain from further animadversions on the quality of tone which results, pointing out only that inequalities of intonation occur rather frequently, and that the odd timbres of the instruments used do nothing to provide the ear with a steadying or compensating element.

Some of the inconsistencies in modern band instrumentation will no doubt have already occurred to the reader. The bandsman is often asked why string basses and harps, certainly not wind instruments, are admitted to the band. The answer is invariably lame, because there is no answer possible without conceding that you might as well have a piano too. The admission of the string bass is, of course, an avowal of the inadequacy of the tubas or of any combination of low instruments in the band, as I have suggested. The use of the harp is justified by the plea of "special effects." On the same grounds, of course, one could argue for the use of the zither. The question remains: When does a wind band cease to be a wind band? Or, really, is the primary idea of the concert band to be a combination of wind instruments, or any combination of instruments differing in composition, tradition and purpose from the orchestra? I suspect that the latter is the case, for reasons which should already be apparent.

There is little doubt that the string bass makes a band sound better; the question is only how far one can continue on that principle. A few violins for the highest register would sound a lot better than the squeaky clarinets, too, and encompass some additional notes. The piano would certainly be of far greater use, in every respect, than the harp, which cannot be heard very well unless indoors, and with an accompaniment of extreme lightness. The string bass aids the band where it is weakest, and it is capable of a sharp *staccato,* which the low wind instruments (except the bassoon) are not. The viola and the 'cello sound in registers where the band already has a large variety of flexible and sonorous instruments; arguments for using these in bands are hence less often heard.

The argument against using the string bass was concisely stated by Sousa, in an article written in about 1900. Sousa wrote: "I do not care for the use of a string contra-bass in a military band. If a string bass, why not a 'cello? And once granted the 'cello, why not the viola and divided violins? In fact, why not become a symphony orchestra all at once? . . . The bass tuba does all and more than a contra-bass can do, is richer, gives fuller and sounder harmonic basis for the volume of tone . . ."

Sousa's view is apparently not held by the majority of bandmasters today, for the string bass has found increasing acceptance in concert bands. Opinion on the use of the 'cello is still strongly divided, and it is actually used in very few American concert bands. The case for its inclusion in the band is stated as follows by Captain George S. Howard, Leader of the Army Air Forces Band: "Since I have had the opportunity of having 'cellos I would never again have a band without them. In our special arrangements they are of course invaluable, but even in the standard stock arrangements they add much by taking the edge off the tuba tones and the baritones. It is true that at times they may not be heard as 'cellos, but the moment they drop out they are heard because of their absence. Then too there are many times when a stock arrangement could be greatly improved by eliminating the baritone and permitting the 'cellos to take the baritone part, if only for a phrase or two."

There is another question on which there is a considerable division of opinion among bandsmen. That question involves the use of wind instruments in complete family groups. Our list of instruments shows a complete family of clarinets, from sopranino to contrabass; a complete family of saxophones, of sarrusophones, of saxhorns, and to some extent of oboes and bassoons. It is the contention of many bandmasters that the complete band must include the complete range of each family of instruments. There are several sides to this question. In the first place, such a usage would presuppose a style of writing in choirs which is nonexistent so far as bands are concerned, although it might very well be effective. It has not, however, been tried since the seventeenth century. To use all these instruments to play the type of harmony music now favored by bandmasters would, I should think, merely accentuate the already too-marked thickness of the band's middle and low registers. To be completely consistent, one should also have a full choir of flutes, as a survival of the consort of recorders. The lower flutes are obsolete in the same way that the consort of recorders is obsolete; they serve no purpose whatsoever in a band, because they cannot be heard, in the first place, and because the few low notes which they could add to the flute range are played very well on B*b* clarinets.

It is obvious that band music has for several centuries tended away from the practice of writing in choirs. The reader has noted the increase in the number of clarinets, for example, as these instruments began to assume the character of leading soprano melody instruments. We now have, as the usual practice, something like the following in a band:

1 or 2 E*b* clarinets
about 20 B*b* clarinets
1 or 2 alto clarinets
1 or 2 bass clarinets

To make a clarinet choir, one would necessarily have to alter these proportions, thinning the middle and strengthening the top and bottom. A similar step would have to be taken with each other family of instruments in the band (it has more nearly been taken with the brasses than with the reeds), but the result would be a band with a weak top voice, entirely unsuited for the performance of nineteenth and twentieth century melodic-harmonic music. It would be ideal for the performance of sixteenth and seventeenth century polyphony!

Nonetheless, it is held by some musicians that the clarinet section of a band is the parallel of the string section of an orchestra. To make an actual parallel, one would have to use a clarinet choir somewhat in the proportions of:

10 first B*b* clarinets
8 second B*b* clarinets
6 alto clarinets
4 bass clarinets
4 contrabass clarinets

and in addition rewrite every piece of band music composed or published up to this time. How this choir would blend with the remaining choirs of the band in the performance of post-seventeenth century music is beyond imagination.

This misconception of the role of the clarinets is quite general. The band has no equivalent of the string choir; if it has any basic group, indeed, it is certainly the brasses rather than the reeds. But the essence of the band is its *mixedness*; and the problem of bandmasters heretofore has been not to isolate various timbres but rather to combine them in the most agreeable total sonority.

Between the theoretical "ideal" of the band and

the practical possibilities of instrumental combination there exists not only a wide divergence, but a complete confusion in terms and aims. The instrumentation of the band can be considered, in a practical sense, only in terms of the *function* the band fulfills, and of the music it expects to perform. Percy Grainger, who has given much serious thought to the problems of the wind band, and whose opinions deserve the most careful attention, feels that no wind band is ideal "without a complete family of . . . sarrusophones" or without bass oboe and heckelphone to complete the family of oboe and English horn. He notes* "that Belgian and French creators and perfectors of wind instruments, such as Sarrus, Charles-Joseph Sax and his son Adolphe, knew what they were doing when they built the various members of the saxophone and sarrusophone families in altitudes corresponding to the natural divisions of the human voice —thereby enabling these instruments to play, without rearrangement, the whole glorious hoard of early European part-songs." It is unquestionably true that these part songs could be played on any complete family of wind instruments; but neither in Sax's time nor in our own have bands included such music in their repertories. Mr. Grainger believes strongly that this music should be revived and played by bands;

* In his preface to the score of *Lads of Wamphray.* New York: Carl Fischer, 1941.

and in making recommendations as to the manner in which it should be played, he is on firm ground. But it is questionable to take the position that the instrumental balance of the wind band should be determined by the qualities of music which it does not perform.

Most theoretical argument concerning the organization of complete choirs within the wind band breaks down on similar ground. We have seen how the group of related instruments was commonly used in the sixteenth and seventeenth centuries, and it should be clear that the usage was determined by the nature of the music as well as by considerations of instrumental consonance and tunability. Were we to revive the instrumental music of Pezel, Schuetz, Gabrieli, Lassus and Frescobaldi as the basis of a modern band repertory, the constitution of the modern band should certainly be altered to suit that music. It is perfectly valid to campaign for a revival of this music (I for one will join Mr. Grainger on that), or to suggest that future band music should be modeled on the sound of many equal voices, but it is not dealing with the question in hand: how can the band sound best in the performance of the music it *now* plays? All arguments on the instrumental make-up of the band must meet a *reductio ad absurdum*: how will it work on the *William Tell* Overture or a Sousa march? For, no matter what our ideas may be on the subject of what bands *should* play, it is apparent that for the present one must deal with what bands *do* play. That the instrumentation of the average modern band might be improved to meet these demands is another possibility, which we shall examine in detail in the following pages.

The weakness of the band in the top register could, it is true, be lessened by the addition of the high clarinets and saxhorns. But the emphasis on building choirs in bands has not been as a rule directed toward their top voices. There is much favor shown for the greater use of the alto clarinet, the tenor horn, the low saxophones, and even the bass trumpet. Yet it seems reasonably clear that the sopranino clarinet would be of markedly greater use in the modern band than the alto, and that the high fluegelhorn would add a more valuable sound than any of the alto or tenor brasses.

The inclusion in the band of the complete family of each instrument might indeed be of some advantage were it practically possible and if many of the instruments were to be used only when specifically necessary. It would give the band limitless possibilities of forming proper combinations for the performance of any type of music. But the inclusion of all these instruments in a normal band (quite aside from the number of players it would involve) would be very much like the practice of never throwing anything out because one never knows when it may come in handy. Meanwhile, one has to find room. To be sure, it would be pleasant to know that one had a bass oboe in the band for the few occasions when a bass oboe might be ideally satisfactory. Meanwhile, once the bass oboe had been admitted, it would be there to stay. The result would be (since most of the instruments in question are, like the bass oboe, middle or low instruments) an additional thickness in the band's massed sound just where it is least needed. It would be impossible, as band tradition exists, to expect so much discretion on the part of composers, arrangers and bandmasters that they would be content to let these instruments be silent when such silence would be desirable.

In most of the music the band plays, such a wealth of instruments, with each family complete, would be of no musical value. There remains the purely practical consideration that no professional band could afford to maintain the number of players necessary, and no amateur band could find them. Even the largest symphony orchestras do not maintain permanently the ensemble of 120 players necessary for a performance of Stravinsky's *Rites of Spring*. Such an ensemble, moreover, even if it could be afforded, would be useless for performances of Mozart, Beethoven and Brahms symphonies. The orchestra follows the sensible practice of having a permanent ensemble which is designed for the performance of *most* of its repertory, using more or fewer players on occasion for specific works. The band, differing completely in practice, has a fixed instrumentation for all works. Hence it is an absolute necessity that the band's instrumentation be determined on the basis of the best possible sound for the largest portion of its repertory.

The concept of instrumentation today, as applied to both orchestras and bands, is an inheritance from the late eighteenth and the nineteenth century. Earlier music, both vocal and instrumental, emphasized the sound pattern made by a weaving of melodic lines characterized by similarity of quality. The unaccompanied chorus of human voices is the ideal example; the string quartet and the string orchestra make music on the same principle, just as did the ancient choir of trombones and cornetts. No idea of instrumental "color" intervened between the musical line on paper and its execution by singer or player. The earliest traditions of instrumentation avoided mixture of timbres, and certainly never included the idea of special "effects" of instrumental color. So little interested were many sixteenth and seventeenth century composers in timbre as such that we find many works written to be performed "by any kind of instruments." Later on, composers began to be interested in instrumentation from a variety of standpoints. Imitative effects were occasionally sought, and solo-voiced accompanied music set the problem of giving emphasis to the single melodic line. One way of setting a melody in relief is to assign it to an instrument of different timbre from those playing the accompaniment. The "mixed consort," still the exception in the seventeenth century, became the basis for the orchestra of the late eighteenth.

That orchestra solved the problem of performing many kinds of music. Its basic string choir could satisfactorily perform any style of part music; its leading violins could, by numerical preponderance, give the melody relief, especially where the style of homophonic writing subordinated the interest of the other parts. But the originality of the new orchestra was in its use of wind instruments. These instruments, by the distinctness of their individual sounds, could be used to call attention to melodic phrases assigned to them and to give *variety* to the repetitions and developments characteristic of classical music.

It is probable that the idea of "color" in instrumentation arose along with the idea of the dramatic, that is, with the development of opera. The most elaborate "coloristic" orchestration of preclassical times was that of Monteverde, the first truly "modern" composer in the sense that he first made use of the devices which have been the stock in trade of all operatic and dramatic composers since his time.

The concept of color, as such, became a part of nineteenth century orchestral music as well as operatic music, when ideas of "drama," theretofore reserved to opera, became widespread in symphonic creation. It is true that isolated examples of color as well as drama may be found in orchestral works before Beethoven, but I cannot find, earlier than Berlioz, a treatise which deals with instrumentation in this sense. Orchestral color generally means the use of various wind instruments, individually or in combination, either for variety alone or for qualities they are supposed to suggest. One need only allude to the adjectives commonly bandied about the wind instruments to understand this concept of color at its most inane level. The "plaintive" oboe is a particularly limp example of nineteenth century sentiment; one cannot imagine Handel, in his lovely oboe sonatas, or Lully, with his raucous army bands of oboes, thinking of the oboe as "plaintive"!

In any case, the band, having borrowed many of its ideas and much of its repertory from the orchestral music of the nineteenth century, absorbed the problem of color in instrumentation. To achieve the effects characteristic of nineteenth century style, the instrumentation of the wind band must allow, at least in theory, for varied tonal colors and contrasting timbres. This is perhaps a more pressing problem than securing the proper balance of instruments for the performance of many-voiced music, for it is a problem pertinent to the type of music actually played. It should be obvious that contrast of color is difficult to achieve in a band, since the wind instruments of the band are massed and do not have the individual speaking qualities which they possess in relation to the orchestra's choir of strings. An individual oboe, for example, makes a very small and unimpressive sound against an accompaniment of mixed clarinets, cornets and saxophones, or whatever similar combination may be called for in the score. Certainly the sound is not comparable to that made by an oboe against an accompaniment of strings or piano, even though the notes may be identical. It is nevertheless possible, with the instrumentation of the modern wind band, to achieve effects of color and contrast. These effects will, of course, be different from those heard in orchestral scores. The points to be emphasized are that the esthetic principle is the same, although the means of realization is different, and that the adjustments necessary to provide color and contrast have been one of the primary considerations in determining the instrumental make-up of the band.

In sum it may be stated that the instrumentation of today's bands represents a compromise rather than an ideal, and a compromise, moreover, which avoids the necessity of defining clearly the direction the band is supposed to take. To achieve every possible variation of tone color would necessitate the inclusion of every available wind instrument. To achieve an absolute balance of voices in each family of instruments would necessitate a further thickening of the band's middle and low registers and an extreme overlapping of voices across the various choirs. An immense number of players would be necessary to satisfy the dozens of theories of how a band should sound and what it should play, and aside from the practical improbability of assembling such a number of skilled players on unusual instruments, it may be doubted that the total effect would be altogether happy. Given both traditions of instrumentation as we have them and the still existing imperfections of many wind instruments, it may be assumed that the constitution of the wind band will continue to evolve. How rationally it will evolve depends partly on the awakened interest of serious composers in the band as a medium of expression, and partly on intelligent thinking by bandmasters about the nature and functions of the band as a musical institution.

CHAPTER V

The Functions of Instruments in the Wind Band

1. *Flutes, Piccolos and Fifes*

The flute in C, most commonly used in modern concert bands, is the same as that used universally in the orchestra. It is therefore a familiar instrument to nonspecialists in band music. The flute in D*b*, once found in bands, is now a rarity; its advantages were negligible or nonexistent, although the theory had it that music in most flat keys was more easily executed on the D*b* instrument. The E*b* flute is sometimes used in amateur bands as a substitute for the E*b* clarinet. The alto flute, pitched in F or G, is a rare instrument, seldom found in either the band or the orchestra. (Stravinsky uses the alto flute in G in the score of *Le Sacre du Printemps.*)

The use of the flute in the band differs considerably from its use in the orchestra. The beauty of the flute is almost entirely lost in the band. As a solo voice, it has insufficient strength, even when the tone is forced; its low notes cannot be heard at all. There are rare exceptions in band music, when an accompaniment is sufficiently subdued and the flute plays in its most brilliant register. (The famous flute solo in the *William Tell* Overture can, for example, be heard in band arrangements; but it does not have the same sound value as the original.) In general, the use of the flute in the wind band is confined to the top register, where it gives valuable assistance to the clarinets. There are other uses, but these may be too technical to be of interest to most readers.

The piccolo, used as an occasional instrument in the orchestra, is a regular and indispensable instrument in a band. Piccolos in C and D*b* are both in common use. It is maintained, as in the case of the flute, that the D*b* piccolo is more generally practical for playing in flat keys. Another claim advanced in favor of its retention is that it possesses greater brilliance than the C instrument. To most people, including the writer, the instruments are indistinguishable in actual sound. The sound, on either D*b* or C piccolo, is strong and shrill; it can be heard even when the full band is playing, and is invaluable in giving a lift to marches or other music of a spirited sort. In some ways, the piccolo does in a band what the flute does in an orchestra. Ingenious composers and arrangers have demonstrated a great number of effective uses for the piccolo beyond those implicit in the original fifelike character of the instrument.

The fife, properly speaking, is not an instrument

of the concert band. It is, however, sometimes used in conjunction with military or parade bands. The military fife is commonly in B*b*.

2. *Clarinets*

There is almost no theoretical limit to the number of clarinets it is possible to construct and use, and an examination of orchestral scores and band music will reveal a very large number which have been used. Six types (or sizes) of clarinet are fairly common in modern wind bands. Most important of these is the clarinet in B*b,* the same instrument that is used in dance orchestras and is most commonly called for in symphonic scores. It is this instrument which is most often designated simply as "the clarinet." Nearly everyone is familiar with the range, quality and flexibility of this versatile instrument, which is a favorite of the serious composer and the jive player alike. In the wind band the B*b* clarinet is the leading melodic instrument among the reeds and woodwinds; there are numerically more of them than of any other instrument. For these reasons, it is often said that the B*b* clarinet is to the band what the violin is to the orchestra. In a very rough sense this can be made to appear true, although there are as many points of functional difference as there are of similarity.

B*b* clarinets in a concert band were at one time divided into first and second clarinets, similar to the division of violins in the orchestra. It is more usual today to find the B*b* clarinets divided into solo, first, second and third parts. (Actually, these are first, second, third and fourth parts; the use of the term "solo" is pointless and misleading.) In practice this often amounts to a division in three parts, as the "solo" and first clarinets may have identical parts. There is no invariable formula for treating the division of the clarinets. Here again, the bandmaster proceeds according to his own theories, usually arranging his clarinets in the manner required by the music to be played, but sometimes in terms of his preconceived notions without regard to the parts as conceived by the composer or arranger.

The clarinets in A*b* and E*b* (sopraninos) and the alto clarinet in E*b* are almost uniquely band instruments, and are less familiar to most listeners. The E*b* sopranino, however, is sometimes used in the orchestra, and its use is on the increase. (It may be noted in scores of Ravel, Stravinsky, Copland, and many others.) In the band, the E*b* sopranino has great and varied uses. The commonest of these is to reinforce the weak flutes and to extend the upward range of the B*b* clarinets. The usual argument against the greater use of the E*b* sopranino is that it is difficult to play in tune and that it has a shrill and unpleasant tone. Granted its importance in giving strength to the band at the top (where, as I have noted, the band is weakest) it seems to me that these two objections should be met and overcome by the development of better players. I have heard the E*b* sopranino (and this is true of the higher A*b* sopranino as well) played in tune with an excellent tone quality. The A*b* sopranino has fallen into complete disuse in the United States, and this I consider especially unfortunate in view of the weaknesses mentioned and the constant addition of instruments to the already overweighted middle registers. Italian and South American bands still use both A*b* and E*b* sopraninos, and play at least as well in tune as most bands in the United States. The local prejudice against these instruments in the concert band is not only unfounded, but tends to deprive the band of a valuable tonal resource.

The E*b* alto clarinet is the band's version of the basset horn in F, used by Mozart. It is pitched a fifth lower than the B*b* clarinet, bearing the same relation to the latter as the viola to the violin. The comparison, however, ends there. In small bands, the alto clarinet is generally absent, while in larger bands there are seldom more than two. Its presence in bands is in large part a matter of concession to the theory that each member of an instrument family should be represented, for although the alto clarinet is in itself an instrument of pleasing quality its presence or absence is of little practical importance. To compare the alto clarinet to the orchestral viola in terms of musical function is, as bands are now constituted, impossible. Its principal duty in the band today is to reinforce, or double, other instruments of the middle register.

The bass clarinet in B*b* is familiar as an orchestral instrument, as it has been in fairly common use since the time of Wagner. Its use in bands is somewhat similar to that of the alto clarinet; since small bands ordinarily are without bass clarinets, and since large bands have one or two, the instrument cannot be compared functionally with any of the strings, or be said to constitute a functional bass to a clarinet choir. The bass clarinet is *part* of the general bass of the woodwind element of the band. It is a more valuable instrument than the alto, as its low notes are extremely rich and true and contribute materially to the sonority of the woodwind bass.

The contrabass clarinet is built both in E*b* and in B*b*, a fifth and an octave, respectively, lower than the bass clarinet. These instruments are used only in a few very large bands. As the band has no instrument, except the contra bassoon, of comparable downward range, the contrabass clarinet can be of value in the production of foundation tones.

3. *Saxophones*

In the one hundred years since its invention, the saxophone has probably had as many detractors as admirers, but like the automobile it seems that it is here to stay, at least in wind bands. Aside from a few experiments, and introductions for the sake of novelty, it has not been generally used in the orchestra. Its popularity derives in part from its distinct tonal quality, and partly from the fact that it is the easiest of all instruments to learn. Its lack of difficulty has contributed greatly to its disrepute, for easy things are generally badly done, and the saxophone is usually poorly mastered. The good saxophone player is still, unfortunately, rare.

Although saxophones have been used in the bands of France since their invention, their introduction into American and British bands has been more recent, and their use less universal, being confined as a rule to the alto and the tenor only. Addition of the baritone has now become quite general, but the soprano and bass saxophones remain comparatively rare. The same objection is made to the soprano saxophone as to the sopranino clarinets, and with about the same justice. The tendency in American bands today is to increase still further the number of alto and tenor saxophones, and to ignore the soprano completely. To the contention that the soprano saxophone cannot be played in tune, the answer might be "let him who is without sin . . ."; in my experience the alto is played out of tune more often than not, but it *can* be played in tune, and so can the soprano. The

French have been able to manage it quite nicely. Ravel, in fact, even demands a *sopranino* saxophone (in F, a fifth higher than the B*b* soprano!) in the score of "Bolero."

Saxophones are without doubt useful in the wind band. They blend well with either brass or woodwind, can be used as melody instruments either in alternation or in conjunction with other instruments, and help give body to the harmony. 'Cellolike passages are often written for the alto and tenor saxophones. The baritone saxophone is normally treated as a sort of alternate bassoon, and forms, with the bass clarinet, a part of the woodwind bass. In a band with good bassoon and bass clarinet players, its importance is somewhat diminished. The bass saxophone has little advantage over the bassoon (its compass extends only one note lower) except for its greater loudness, and has the disadvantage of sounding heavy and sluggish. A contrabass saxophone has been built and used, but is still to be classed as an oddity.

The general loudness of the saxophones gave their inventor the idea that bands using enough of them could dispense with oboes, bassoons and possibly even clarinets. The idea was fortunately not taken quite literally; the saxophone is less flexible than the other woodwinds, and more difficult to play softly, so that while it adds to the resources of a band it does not adequately substitute for the older instruments. Its tone is sufficiently distinctive to justify its use on the basis of "color" variety alone.

4. *Double Reeds*

(Oboes, English Horn, Heckelphone, Bassoons, Sarrusophones)

The modern oboe, used in the symphony orchestra and in the concert band, is an instrument of rather different character from the oboe used in early military music. As its tone has become more delicate, the nature of its use in the band has changed entirely. The seventeenth century oboe, as we have seen, was the leading woodwind of town and military bands; its tone was much more strident and coarse than that of the modern instrument. As the clarinet came to the fore, and engaged the attention of composers and bandsmen alike, the oboe became a more specialized instrument, less generally a utilitarian voice in woodwind harmony and more valued for the uniqueness of its timbre.

The oboes and bassoons descend from a composite family of instruments known as shawms (or schalmeys) and pommers. All of them were wooden instruments of conical bore, played with a double reed. Apart from this basic similarity, the two groups of instruments were differentiated by their timbres, a distinction which has carried down to present-day oboes and bassoons. Although it is common today to refer to the oboes and bassoons as being a single family, it may be noted that Lully's oboe bands consisted of discant, alto, tenor and bass oboes, and not oboes and bassoons, or pommers. The true family of oboes, as constituted today, includes the oboe, English horn, heckelphone and bass oboe. The English horn, frequently used in bands, is in F, a fifth lower than the oboe; the heckelphone is a baritone, one octave lower than the oboe, called for by Richard Strauss in *Salome,* but uncommon in either orchestra or band. It replaces the bass oboe, which is now obsolete. (The oboe d'amore, a minor third lower than the oboe, has not been used in bands; it is called for in many ancient and some modern orchestral scores.)

The oboe and English horn are not indispensable in the wind band today. The number of clarinets overpowers the oboe tone in full passages and eliminates the need for the oboe in upper harmonies. Both oboe and English horn have hence come to be useful in the band mainly as solo voices. Here the problem is one of bringing them into relief against the timbre of saxophones and clarinets, both of which are stronger. When properly used, the oboe and English horn can be heard effectively in the wind band, and thus their retention is more than amply justified.

The bassoon was at one time the only bass of any value among the woodwinds. Its importance has diminished considerably so far as the modern wind band is concerned, and to some extent it has been allowed to revert to its real character as a *tenor* instrument. As we have seen, Sax felt that it could be eliminated entirely. It has, however, been retained, except in small bands, and it is still, despite improvements in other instruments, the most useful of the lower reeds. One disability of the bassoon in the band is that, because of the weight of the other wind instruments, it is difficult to write effective solo passages for it such as those which occur frequently in orchestral scores. The contra bassoon, found only in large concert bands, is a very valuable foundation instrument, although the difficulty of finding players restricts its use.

Sarrusophones are a family of double-reed instruments found only in wind bands; in many countries, notably England and the United States, they are not in general use. The instrument family follows closely the model of the saxophones, ranging from a soprano in E*b* to a contrabass in E*b*. The inventor, a French bandmaster named Sarrus, felt as Sax did, that some new instrument was needed to replace the too-weak oboes and bassoons in the modern band. The sarrusophones are, with some modifications, oboes and bassoons in brass instead of wood, built in the "band keys" of E*b* and B*b*. The range of the sarrusophones is about two and one-half octaves, comparing favorably with the oboe and English horn in this respect, but lacking about an octave of the bassoon's range. Thus at least two sarrusophones are needed to replace the bassoon in its entire range. Sarrus, however, again like Sax, envisioned the adoption of the entire family of his instruments, in order to cover the entire compass with notes of similar timbre.

The sarrusophones have a louder and coarser sound than oboes and bassoons, and probably approximate the tones of the ancient schalmeys and pommers more closely than any other modern instrument. The contrabass has had greater acceptance than any of the other sarrusophones, as it has been used in both bands and orchestras (in the latter, notably by Saint-Saëns and Massenet) to replace the contra bassoon.

5. *The Brasses*

Of the brasses used in the wind band, the French horn, trumpet, trombone, and to some extent the tuba, are more familiar as orchestral instruments. All the others are more or less uniquely band instruments. The brasses are the real core of the band, forming a complete and solid harmony in which all timbres blend well. They are capable of performing with both extreme loudness and extreme softness, and lack only lightness of tone and facility in very rapid passages to make comparison with the string choir of the orchestra inevitable. Comparison with any part of the orchestra breaks down, however, for the reason that the band brasses not only must do all that the orchestral brasses do, but also the work done in the orchestra by many strings and woodwinds. The tuba, in the band, is not used to reinforce the string basses; it *is* the bass. The trumpet and trombone are not reserved for climaxes or special effects; they play most of the time in a band, even when they do not have a leading part. These examples are of course rough; what is to be emphasized is that without the brasses there is no band at all.

For purposes of approximate classification, the band brasses may be divided according to range as follows:

Top: cornets, trumpets, fluegelhorns
Upper Middle: French horns, alto horns
Lower Middle: trombones, tenor horns, baritones
Bass: euphonium, bass trombone, tubas

These instruments overlap considerably, and further subdivisions must be noted. The band has two to six, and often more, of each brass instrument, and it is the general practice to write in parts for each instrument. Thus, depending on the arranger or composer, the 2nd and 3rd cornets, or the fluegelhorns, may be playing with or below one or more of the horns or trombones; the horns may be, and probably are, divided into two to four parts, and the trombones in three more. Were it not for the fact that these brass instruments are differentiated by their qualities and limitations, and were they not functionally distinct in the band, one would be tempted to say that there are almost too many of them. In some cases, one would be completely justified in making this statement. As a rule, however (and as with every rule, there are exceptions), each brass instrument has a well-defined place.

The total number of individual brass *parts,* as distinct from brass *instruments,* is somewhat as follows, using the recommendations of the American Bandmasters Association as a basis:

solo or 1st cornet in B*b*	1st trumpet in B*b*
2nd cornet in B*b*	2nd trumpet in B*b*
3rd cornet in B*b*	
1st fluegelhorn in B*b* (ad lib)	
2nd fluegelhorn in B*b* (ad lib)	
1st horn in F or alto in E*b*	
2nd horn in F or alto in E*b*	
3rd horn in F or alto in E*b*	
4th horn in F or alto in E*b*	
1st trombone	baritone
2nd trombone	euphonium
3rd trombone (bass)	tubas

Thus we have a minimum of 15 separate brass parts, of which at least 12 are considered essential. Bands of most countries, aside from the United States and England, usually have still more parts, as altos are distinct from French horns, and parts are provided for tenor horn and a sopranino, either trumpet or fluegelhorn. The reader can now see easily why comparison with orchestral brass or strings breaks down.

According to function, the following rough attempt at division may be helpful. Melody-carrying instruments are primarily the cornet (or fluegelhorn), baritone (or euphonium), and trombone, depending on the character and range of the melody. Instruments used principally for harmony (inner parts) and rhythm (after beats and accents) are the horns, trumpets and altos. It will be observed that the leading parts are in general not taken by the "classical" brass instruments of the orchestra (trumpet, French horn and trombone) but by the saxhorns and their derivatives. A word on the saxhorn family is therefore in order.

The saxhorns are brass instruments made with a relatively wide conical bore, giving them all a less incisive tone than that of the trumpet, trombone or French horn. They were designed originally not as improvements of the trumpet family, but to replace the old key bugles and ophicleides, which in turn had displaced the zinken, post horns, and serpents. The saxhorns, with Sax's mechanical improvements in valves and tube curvature, are reliable as to intonation and relatively easy to play. Because of their wide bore, they produce the lower notes of the harmonic series with facility, whereas the trumpet and horn are more effective in the upper notes. It has been held that Sax sacrificed quality of tone in his instruments for facility of tone production and accuracy of intonation over a fairly wide compass. A certain coarseness of tone is in most textbooks ascribed to the saxhorns, and advanced as the reason why they have never been adopted in the orchestra. Whatever the merits of this argument, the saxhorns have been one of the foundations of the modern band, and have made brass instruments accessible to amateurs as they never were previously.

The structure of Sax's family of horns brings us to one of the oddities of nomenclature which makes a study of band instruments so confusing. In Sax's terminology (a correct one, by the way) the instruments are as follows:

soprano fluegelhorn or bugle in E*b*
alto fluegelhorn in B*b*
tenor horn in E*b* (called also althorn, *not* alto horn)
baritone horn in B*b*
euphonium in B*b*
tubas in E*b*, B*b*

What should be noted is that, correctly speaking, the B*b* fluegelhorn (and its derivative, the B*b* cornet), treated in the band as soprano instruments, are actually *altos*; the E*b* horn (commonly called E*b* alto) is actually a *tenor*; what is today called the tenor horn (in B*b*) is actually a baritone, distinct from the baritone proper only by a slightly narrower bore. American and English bands, lacking the true soprano, have simply moved the whole nomenclature up one notch. Thus, when the E*b* fluegelhorn is used, it is called a sopranino.

The cornet is not a true saxhorn. Theoretically at least, it is midway between the fluegelhorn and the trumpet, with greater flexibility than the latter and a more "refined" tone than the former. Its advantages and disadvantages have been the subject of much dispute; for a time it was used in the orchestra, often arbitrarily, at the discretion of trumpet players, but it is now almost universal practice to insist on trumpets for the performance of orchestral trumpet parts. Conversely, it is now the usual practice, since the cornet has come into disfavor in the orchestra, to use trumpets even when cornets are specified, as in a number of scores by French composers.*

As the saxhorns were devised at a time when the trumpet, cornet and horn were already in use, and as bandsmen in general have never been able to make up their minds whether the saxhorns were to replace other instruments or be added to the ensemble, a great deal of overlapping and sometimes duplication is

* In the score of *Petrouchka* (1911) Stravinsky calls for two cornets and two trumpets. Students interested in learning how the cornet is used by a master of instrumentation are urged to examine the same composer's score, *Histoire du Soldat* (1918).

found in the complete modern wind band. It is best therefore, in order to clarify certain band problems, to discuss the parallelisms and differences in each group of band brasses.

A. Cornets, Trumpets and Fluegelhorns

The trumpet and cornet are today more similar than they have been at any stage of their history. We have earlier noted the immense differences between the two instruments in the seventeenth century, differences which were functional as well as structural. The zinke, from which the cornet is functionally, if not structurally, descended, was a wooden instrument with finger holes. It was played with a deep cup-shaped mouthpiece. Its completely conical bore gave it a powerful tone entirely different from the brilliant sound of the trumpet. The natural trumpet was almost completely evolved, as we know it today, by the seventeenth century. It was a metal tube, of cylindrical bore for most of its length, played with a rather shallow or hemispherical mouthpiece. The trumpet was used for fanfares and military music of a brilliant character; the zinke was far more of a popular and utilitarian instrument. Aside from its use in town bands, it was used by composers such as Bach and Gluck, generally to reinforce vocal parts. It was, in other words, a *melody* instrument at all times.

The zinke began to disappear in the eighteenth

century partly because it was difficult to blow and partly because of the improvements in the fabrication of metal horns. Both the cornet and the fluegelhorn were the result of the effort to make the metal bugle or the post horn as useful for melody playing as the zinke had been. In 1810 an English bandmaster named Halliday devised a system of holes and keys for obtaining chromatic degrees. The key bugle, as it was known, became widely popular, especially for use in bands. Valves, instead of keys, were devised for the bugle and horn about 1813, and patented in 1815 in Germany. The modifications of tubing which resulted from the adoption of valves, however, changed the instrument from one of pure bugle type to one of mixed conical and cylindrical bore. This instrument became known as the cornet-à-pistons, and by about 1835 had almost completely supplanted the key bugle.

The fluegelhorn is the result of Sax's adaptation of valves to an instrument of purer bugle type with respect to bore, and is hence a more faithful descendant of the zinke than the modern cornet. (Sax called his instrument a saxhorn; the name "fluegelhorn" arose in Germany from the practice of having the players of this instrument placed at the ends, or wings, of lines while on the march. In France it is known as a *bugle*.) Valves were introduced at about this same period for the trumpet. In each case, the introduction of valves resulted in some modification of the character of the natural instrument. The result has been, since the middle of the nineteenth century, progressively to de-emphasize the difference between the instruments, and to tend to make them appear variations of one type of instrument. Today they are theoretically constructed as follows: the trumpet of two-thirds cylindrical and one-third conical bore, played with a shallow mouthpiece; the cornet of one-third cylindrical and two-thirds conical bore, played with a deep mouthpiece; the fluegelhorn like the cornet, but of wider and more nearly all conical bore.

A question which has always agitated bandsmen involves the use of these three instruments. Most European bands have always used all three; most English and American bands have used cornets and trumpets only. Any number of arguments are adduced in defense of various theories about the proper employment of the instruments, but all are of course based on the assumption that there is a real difference of character among them. This is true to a much smaller degree than one would believe, after hearing some of the heated discussions of the subject. The arguments would be more interesting if the instruments were more like their prototypes, but the cornet and trumpet, as manufactured today, are so little different that arguing about which to use, or how, is in reality splitting hairs. The cornet is becoming of smaller bore and more and more resembles the trumpet. Mouthpieces of the shallow trumpet type are generally used for both trumpet and cornet. The tones produced on each are almost interchangeable, depending on the player rather than on the instrument. My contention is therefore that while *originally* the cornet and trumpet were vastly different, no such difference exists today; a skillful player can produce a "cornet" tone on a trumpet, or a "trumpet" tone on a cornet, with equal facility, and most people will never know which instrument is being played.

The fluegelhorn is still theoretically of different character, and has become less modified in the direction of the trumpet than has the cornet. But how little the theoretical character of these instruments is understood may be seen from the chart of instrumentation officially recommended for American high school bands, Class C. Two fluegelhorns are included, with the advice that, if they are not available, two *trumpets* may be used as substitutes. This is of course completely confused so far as the theoretical character of the instruments is concerned; the substitution of cornets would at least be closer.

From theoretical differentiation to actual practice is a long way. The use of the fluegelhorn, in addition to the cornet and trumpet, is becoming more general in American bands. By and large, however, it is used as a sort of 4th or 5th cornet, or even as an extra trumpet. It is customary to consider the cornet as the main melody and solo instrument of the band, and the trumpet as a fanfare or accent instrument. These differences actually exist only as a manner of writing the music; the separation of the parts is an acknowledgment, although a confused one, of the *theoretical* difference of the instruments in actual sound.

The adoption of all three instruments continues the tendency toward overstrengthening the wind band in certain registers. Few compositions or arrangements require all of the brass strength, harmonic or melodic, represented by the array of cornets, trumpets and fluegelhorns characteristic of many present-day combinations. European bands compensate at least in part for this overstrength by using one or more *high* fluegelhorns or trumpets in E*b*. It would appear extremely reasonable for American bands to follow suit, but for some reason few moves have been made in this direction.

B. French Horns and Eb Altos

The E*b* alto, one of the true saxhorns, resembles a large fluegelhorn stood on end. It has approximately the same range as the French horn, but a far less individual sound or timbre. It is infinitely easier to play than the French horn, and it produces a louder and coarser tone. For these reasons it has sometimes been used, particularly in small bands and in amateur organizations, to replace the French horn.

The French horn, like the oboe and flute, does not have the same sound value in a band as in an orchestra. The weight of cornets, trumpets and various saxhorns alters the relative effect considerably. In the orchestra, the horn is one of the most often-used and satisfactory solo instruments; it is rarely so used with success in the band. The massed horns in the orchestra seem to have great power; in the band their weight is little against the other brass. The French horn in the band is used principally for rhythmic punctuation or sustained inner harmonies. It *can* be used, and beautifully, as a solo instrument in the band, but solos of a hornlike character are more often assigned to the fuller toned and more reliable baritone (see below).

The alto cannot successfully substitute for the horn as a solo instrument, but for afterbeats in marches, and for the production of staccato notes, it is sometimes more satisfactory than the horn. Many bands include both instruments. In European band arrangements, the parts for horns and altos are distinct; in America and England, however, the same parts are generally used for either instrument or both. When altos and horns are *simultaneously* used on the same parts, thickness of sound inevitably results.

One variant of the E*b* alto, used almost entirely in amateur bands, is the mellophone. This instrument is simply an E*b* alto, constructed in the shape of a French horn rather than in normal saxhorn style. Its advantages over the alto are those of appearance only.

C. Baritones, Euphoniums, Trombones and Tenor Horns

One of the arresting inconsistencies of modern band instrumentation lies in the fact that many bandmasters insist on representation of every variety of saxhorn or clarinet or saxophone, yet are content to use only the tenor trombone, completely ignoring the alto and the bass of the species. That is not to say that every instrument of every species *should* be used; but it is nonetheless inconsistent to discriminate against one family.

The trombone's uses in the band differ mainly in quantity rather than quality from its uses in the orchestra. It is an impressive instrument when used melodically, and it blends with almost any other instrument in harmony. The slide gives to the trombone certain advantages and limitations which more than anything else determine the nature of its use, in either the band or the orchestra. The valve trombone, now rarely used in American bands, represents an attempt to combine trombone timbre with saxhorn facility. By the addition of valves, however, the quality of the slide trombone is slightly altered.

The baritone and euphonium, of approximately the same range as the tenor and bass trombone, are purely band instruments, although the euphonium has on rare occasions been included in orchestra scores. The baritone and euphonium differ in that the euphonium is of wider bore, giving greater volume to the lower notes, and is equipped with an extra valve which lowers the compass an augmented fourth. The tenor horn differs from the baritone by having a somewhat smaller bore, giving it a lighter quality. Aside from the few extra low notes of the euphonium, all three instruments are of the same range; in practice the distinctions between them are often ignored, and parts are written interchangeably.

Although these instruments have not generally been adopted by the orchestra, and although they are criticized on the ground of coarseness of tone quality, they are more pleasing to most ears than any of the other saxhorns. However one estimates their quality, they are indispensable in wind bands. They are easy to play, capable of rapid execution, reasonably reliable as to intonation, and adequate as to volume. To them, in the band, are often assigned passages comparable to those played by 'cellos in the orchestra. Horn solos, or vocal passages, also are often given, in band transcriptions, to the baritone. Because of its volume and its smoothness, the baritone is a very effective solo or melody instrument in the band, having a sound value comparable in many respects to the horn in the orchestra. It lacks the dash and brilliance of the trombone for certain types of music, but in other respects it may be used in a similar manner. The baritone and euphonium blend equally well with the woodwinds and with the other brasses.

D. *Tubas*

The tuba is the bass of the saxhorn family and is familiar through its increasingly general use in the orchestra. Tubas used in bands are of several sizes, ranging from a small B*b* tuba, which actually has the same compass as the euphonium, to the E*b* and BB*b* tubas, a fifth and an octave lower respectively. In the previous chapter, certain observations were made concerning the tubas in general, to which little need be added. A special type of tuba often used in bands is the helicon. This is a tuba constructed to encircle the body of the player, with the weight resting on the player's shoulder. It is obviously useful for marching bands. The sousaphone, devised by John Philip Sousa, is a helicon with an adjustable bell which may be turned to project the sound in any desired direction. The sousaphone is more used in bands than any other model of tuba.

6. *Percussion Instruments*

As most of the percussion instruments used in the band are also used in the orchestra, the difference is principally one of why and how they are used. The band percussion is, of course, functional in origin; the drums beat rhythm for marching or for various calls connected with military ceremonies. The survival of these functions in the concert band tends to produce something of an overabundance of percussion in the performances of nonmilitary music. The idea of noise as a desideratum in band music persists; and it is of course undeniable that the percussion instruments are useful in this respect. That they are useful in many other respects, and that the effectiveness of their use sometimes increases in inverse proportion to the quantity of noise produced, is a thought worth considering.

The basic percussion instruments of a concert band are timpani, bass drum, snare drum and cymbals. To these are added, as in the orchestra, triangle, tambourine, chimes of various sorts, wood blocks and other special instruments as desired or as called for in the score. The cymbal, in the band, is used with the bass drum, especially in marches, though the usage unfortunately carries over to nonmilitary music at times as well. Metal-bar instruments, such as the lyre or the glockenspiel, have been popular in bands since the vogue of Turkish music in the eighteenth century. Xylophones, marimbas, vibraphones and other melodic percussion instruments are in wide use. Parts for these instruments are not yet considered "standard" in wind band arrangements, so that they cannot at this moment be considered more than "special effects," to be used at the discretion of the bandmaster or when specifically called for in the score.

7. *Stringed Instruments*

No discussion of the instruments of the concert band is complete without mention of the string bass, the violoncello and the harp. These instruments are completely familiar to everyone who has heard or seen an orchestra, and a discussion of their place in the wind band may be found in the preceding chapter of this book. We may reiterate that the string bass and 'cello are "helpers" only in the wind band, not essential elements of the ensemble as they are in the orchestra. The use of the harp in the band is entirely a matter of opinion; it is so often badly abused in the orchestra (many movie scores are not considered complete without a large amount of whooping and gushing on the harp) that bandsmen at least have a horrible example of "special effects" to which they can point in self-defense.

CHAPTER VI

Band Arrangements and Transcriptions: Some Theatrical and Practical Problems

WITH THE BAND, the starting point is always the given combination of instruments. Most of the music heard at band concerts is transcribed from works written for the orchestra or other instrumental mediums. The music the band plays must be written or arranged for the instruments known to be present in the band or, as in the case of American school bands, for the instruments theoretically present in prescribed numbers. The composer or arranger has little choice in the matter. Whatever the character of the music may be, there must be a part for every instrument. If the arranger wishes to omit a second alto saxophone part, or to add a part for high E*b* trumpet, he must resist his inclination or accept the fact that his work will probably not be played. The first psychological requisite in a band arranger is the ability to accept realistically the knowledge that in band music the instruments are not chosen for their appropriateness to the music, but that the music must be adapted to fit the instruments.

This situation gives rise to a number of technical and esthetic problems which do not exist in orchestral music. Basically, the problem of the arranger is to make a given piece of music sound as satisfactory as possible when played by a given combination of wind instruments. There are no set rules as to how he can accomplish this; many arrangers have formulas, and many textbooks suggest methods, but the good arranger considers each piece of music as a separate problem.

The normal process of composing is to choose instruments to fit one's needs. In that respect, arranging is the reverse of composing. It is true that the modern orchestra is somewhat standardized, and that the composer writing an orchestral work knows what instruments make up the normal orchestra. But—and this is a very important *but*—he does not *have* to use every instrument, and he may call for any combination of available instruments he wishes. The history of orchestration is not the history of what this or that conductor or association decided, but the history of what various composers called for in their music. The composition of the orchestra, as I have pointed out before, is determined by the music. It would be considered absurd to have a Haydn symphony, written for 2 oboes, 2 horns, 2 bassoons, and strings (perhaps some 30 players in all), performed by the orchestra of Richard Strauss or Maurice Ravel, just as it would rightly be considered impossible to have the music of Strauss or Ravel played by the orchestra of Haydn or Mozart.

The orchestral composer (and to an extent even the orchestral arranger) has a power of discretion as to instrumentation, and, most important, he is still considered the person with the greatest right to be heard on the subject. Whether he wishes to expand or to contract the size, or alter the proportions of the orchestra, he is thought to have a right to do so. He may even write an orchestral composition without violins. In short, his instrumentation is regarded as a part of the total concept of composition, but not as an end in itself.

It is true that arrangements are made for amateur orchestras, theater orchestras, and other small groups. In these, as a rule, some attempt is made to preserve the relative values of the original. The general tendency is toward reduction and simplification rather than enlargement. It is also clearly understood that such arrangements, like piano reductions, are substitutes for the real thing, and that the real thing is what came from the pen of the composer.

On the other hand, the position taken by some bandsmen is that the real thing (that is, the score as written by the composer) is not very much a matter to be concerned about; the important consideration is how the given piece sounds when the band plays it.

The band plays Haydn, Mozart, Wagner, Sousa, Sibelius, Gershwin, Bach, Delibes, or a fantasy on "The Old Oaken Bucket," with the same instrumentation. In effect, this position implies that the character of the original instrumentation is to be forgotten: a *new* character is given the work by translation into a different medium. This position is wholly tenable; it is the only one that makes sense in a consideration of band music. It is impossible to talk about band music as an *imitation* of orchestral music without being forced to the conclusion that band music is altogether pointless.

There is great misunderstanding of this position both among music listeners and among bandsmen. One often hears bandsmen speak of arrangements in terms of similarity to orchestral sound, or take pride in the fact that the clarinets in such-and-such a passage "sounded just like fiddles." Conversely, one often hears listeners remark that the clarinets, alas, *don't* sound like fiddles. The realistic position on band arrangements is, in my opinion, to ask why in the name of anything *should* clarinets sound like fiddles, or a good band sound like an orchestra? If band music has any place in the world, it is precisely because it is band music, and not because it is a makeshift for something else.

I have been at some pains in preceding chapters to point out that the band does not actually have any

he United States Navy Band, Lt. Charles Brendler, USN, Leader, CWO Richard E. Townsend, Assistant Leader.

he United States Army Air Forces Band, Capt. George S. Howard, AC, Leader, 'OJG John R. Barrows, Assistant Leader. Note unusual placing of flutes, bassoons and 'cellos.

equivalent for the string section of an orchestra, and that many instruments have different sound values in a band. It becomes therefore the problem of the arranger not to imitate, or reproduce, the sound of the original orchestral score, but to re-create the music *as a band score.* It should be in terms of its sound as band music, not in terms of its nearness or remoteness from its sound as orchestral music, that it should be judged.

An example will illuminate this point more perhaps than several paragraphs of theoretical argument. Some years ago, Erik W. G. Leidzén, one of the best band arrangers in the United States, transcribed the Finale of Dvorak's *New World* Symphony for band. Mr. Leidzén was criticized for his treatment of a certain passage which, in the orchestral original, is played by the solo clarinet. In his band transcription, Mr. Leidzén wrote this passage for the cornet. The critics maintained that this was "not like the original," that "it was unnecessary to make the change," and that it was wrong for this reason or that. In so arguing, they showed that what they wanted was not band music but a substitute for orchestra music. As a result, the arranger rewrote the passage, scoring it for clarinet, but indicating a "cue," or alternate scoring, for the cornet. Mr. Leidzén's original reasoning was completely correct: the clarinet, playing a solo passage in the orchestra, has an entirely different value from that which the clarinet possesses against the other numerous clarinets of the band. The musical effect (one might even say the musical truth) of the passage is far better realized in the band by giving the solo in question to an instrument of distinct and different timbre, such as the cornet. Mr. Leidzén's first solution showed his awareness that the band must speak in its own idiom.

This example is a pertinent one, but a number of others could of course be cited. If the solo in question had been played by the viola in the orchestra, the transcriber could have assigned it to any instrument in the band without arousing any comment, since the band does not include violas. The fact that both orchestra and band include clarinets is a misleading similarity and means absolutely nothing, as I have tried to show; the functions of the instrument in each group are entirely different. I venture to cite as another example my own transcription of the *Eight Russian Folk Songs* of Liadov. In the third of these, the orchestral scoring is principally for the string choir, with the 'cellos divided into four parts. Since I have always held that the orchestral strings are *not* paralleled by the clarinet and reed section of a band, I sought in my band transcription for that combination of instruments which would give the *homogeneity* and *smoothness* characteristic of middle and low strings. That homogeneity and smoothness I found in the full brass section of the band, and I so transcribed the music. The fact that I received no special criticism for so doing is perhaps attributable to the fact that the original score is less familiar than that of the *New World* Symphony.

It is in connection with familiar orchestral music that memory and recognition further complicate the esthetic problem of band transcriptions. Let us take, for example, a Mozart overture, written for an orchestra tiny by our standards, and transcribed to be played by a wind band of 80 players. It is possible that someone completely unfamiliar with the overture, or with Mozart's music in general, might find the hypothetical band arrangement neither better nor worse than any other piece of band music. On the other hand, a listener familiar with the original might find the arrangement objectionable on a number of grounds. His arguments will in all probability be comparative: that the arrangement lacks all the essential qualities of the original, that it sounds lumpy instead of delicate, heavy instead of light, ponderous instead of gay; his conclusion is likely to be that the work should never have been arranged for band. He will be as dissatisfied with the band version as most bandsmen would be with a string quartet arrangement of *The Stars and Stripes Forever,* and may even consider the artistic result approximately the same as trying to play the Kreutzer

Sonata on a slide whistle. He will, in short, claim that the band is not a suitable medium for that style of music, just as the bandsmen would claim that a string quartet is hardly the medium for playing marches. Both parties are arguing from the character of the music, and not from the quality of the arrangement. In both cases they are probably, though not necessarily, right in defending a legitimate idea of *appropriateness* of certain specific music for a given medium.

This appropriateness is an arguable quality. Certainly there is much music which, if transcribed for band, would approach burlesque or parody. Taste is hard to define or to delimit, but it is important that it be exercised. Transcription as such is an old and honorable musical practice, but like everything else it can be abused and made disreputable. It happens that in band music transcription is a major issue, because without transcribed music the bulk of the band's serious repertory vanishes. Common sense and a bit of musical discretion are certainly the best guides in determining the suitability of music for transcription or arrangement. The important consideration is not that what is transcribed for band necessarily be good music, but that it make good band music. Much of the standard orchestral repertory makes very good band music without reference to its quality as orchestral music or to the peculiarities of its original instrumentation. If a work is successfully and intelligently recast in band idiom, neither merely imitating nor grossly parodying the orchestra, it will sound well as a band piece. The best sort of band arrangement or transcription is clearly one which does not constantly remind the listener that it is an arrangement; it is one in which the music and the instrumental medium have been so successfully combined that the total impression is one of naturalness.

Whether or not one prefers the original is another matter, not totally irrelevant to our discussion. Preference for the original implies acquaintance with the original of course; it is precisely on this ground that band music at present faces something of a dilemma. Not many years ago it could be claimed with complete justice that the band concert was the means through which the standard orchestral overtures and stock pieces were made available to the masses of people. With the radio and the phonograph, the band no longer is the sole purveyor of this type of music to the general public. I for one join heartily with those critics of the band who can see no sense in the concert band's playing Beethoven symphonies and other music which orchestras not only play better, but play *often* enough for all who care to hear them. The orchestra today is also a medium of mass entertainment; it has taken over a good portion of a field that once was the band's exclusively. There is, however, still plenty of territory for the band. There is the vast amount of orchestral music which the orchestras seldom or never perform; this includes not only works which may be classified as minor, or rare, but hundreds of works which audiences welcome, but which are considered too unassuming or stale for the orchestral concert. There is much good honest music there, enough for several years of concerts, with no intermissions.

We have so far been concerned exclusively with band transcriptions from the orchestral repertory, as these loom largest in the views of bandsmen and of the public. The band draws to a smaller degree, though still considerably, on works written for the piano, for organ, or for miscellaneous instrumental combinations. Here of course the problem of "imitation" does not exist, and we may assume that there is no more exception to band arrangements of such music than there is to orchestral versions of Liszt's Hungarian Rhapsodies or Bach's larger fugues.* Quite a good bit of orchestral music was originally written for the piano and arranged for orchestra later by the composers. (Ravel, for example, did this with many of his works.) The fact that a composer

* So much of Bach's music has been arranged, and rather elaborately arranged, that one has the feeling that Bach will be listed in the musical dictionaries of the future as "a talented collaborator of Leopold Stokowski and others."

has made or approved a transcription from one medium to another does not imply that he prefers the transcription, or even that he considers it as satisfactory as the original; it does imply, however, that the composer concedes its right to coexist with the original. It is this right to coexistence that justifies most band transcriptions. There are here, as with orchestral music, practical and common-sense limits as to what can or should be done. The difference is principally that the basis for comparison with the original is not so obvious, nor so often disadvantageous, and that the arranger is likely to work more naturally in a band idiom with less thought of imitating orchestral balances and effects.

It is possible to discuss the question of transcription interminably from the point of view of artistic practice; there are innumerable opinions, ranging from those of the purist, who opposes any form of transcription whatsoever, to those of the thoroughgoing utilitarian, who seems to feel that any piece of music should be adaptable to any performing medium. Somewhere beyond any extreme is Hollywood, which feels that a composer is only a composer, but an arranger can really make things sound. If this sentiment were confined to Hollywood it might be more amusing; there are some indications, alas, that "arranging" as such is becoming a national blight. I should imagine that the graves of

Chopin and Tchaikovsky can now be photographed only with a moving-picture camera. We may fear the day when all legitimate music will be "improved"; I note it here because it is not irrelevant to certain tendencies in band music and band arranging. These tendencies are toward the fancy rather than the straightforward, the elaborate rather than the simple, and the disguised rather than the honest. They can be met only by the exercise of taste to which we have made reference.

I have touched upon only a few of the more striking aspects of the artistic problems of arranging and transcribing music for band. It is important for the band student to know that these problems exist and that more than one view of them is possible. They constitute a fundamental aspect of the nature of the concert band. I have tried to state the case briefly before proceeding to the other aspect of the matter: the practical problems of band transcription.

Nearly all the famous bandmasters of the past hundred years either themselves arranged much of the music played by their bands, or have had other men make arrangements especially for their use. Wieprecht, as we have seen, was one of the first to arrange classic works (whole symphonies, in fact) for band; Gilmore built up a large library of his own arrangements, and arrangements made for him; Sir Daniel Godfrey was an illustrious arranger as well as a great bandmaster. The same combination of activity characterized Vessella in Italy, Zimmermann in Austria, Sellenick and Balay in France, and nearly all the internationally celebrated bandmasters. In the United States, Sousa and Goldman both have built up huge libraries of music specially arranged for their bands by the most expert craftsmen available. In every instance it was recognized as desirable to have arrangements made for a specific band with its own instrumentation. Such arrangements are not interchangeable; they are distinguished not only by national differences in band instrumentation, but by personal idiosyncrasy as well.

This is of course not merely a sensible practice; it is an ideal one. It is taking fact, not theory, and dealing with it. Under such conditions, the arranger knows not only exactly what instruments (and how many of each) he has available, but he knows also the capabilities of the players on each. Nothing is left to chance or improvisation. Balance and tone quality can be calculated, and music can be selected and arranged in an intelligent manner. The fact that a given piece will sound differently when played by different bands is inherent in the nature both of "arranged" music and of band music.

Opposed to this is the theory of the universally

practical band arrangement, which is entirely a matter of convenience, and to some extent of necessity. It is, as we have seen, impossible to arrange a work so that it can be played equally well by a band in South America, a band in Russia, a band in France, and a band in the United States. It is also impossible to arrange a work so that it will sound equally well when played by a band of 30 players and a band of 90 players. This is, however, what is attempted in the commercial arrangements which are the basic diet of most bands today. Any one such arrangement may be a splendid job for a given band, for which it was perhaps originally designed, but no arrangement can be so flexible as to cover all the varying instrumentations and varying abilities for which it is supposed to provide. This is the major problem of band arranging as a practical matter.

Many bandmasters in the United States and abroad have campaigned for the adoption of a universal band instrumentation as a solution, but no practical steps in this direction have been taken and it seems unlikely that any ever will be taken. National traditions are, as we have seen, very strong, and each bandmaster as a rule remains firmly convinced that his preferred instrumentation is the best. It is foolish to speak, as some do, when discussing a universal band instrumentation, of a standard or universal orchestra. The orchestra is international, it is true, but only because Beethoven, Mozart and Tchaikovsky are international. Each composer uses a somewhat different orchestra and may vary it from one work to another. The performing orchestras, in no matter what country, perform these works with the instruments specified in the score. The fact that a symphony orchestra may have 100 or more players on the payroll does not mean that the entire 100 are used in a Haydn symphony.

The band has never operated on this principle. It plays each piece of music with exactly the same combination of instruments. It has no great literature which, as a matter of artistic necessity, it must perform with a stated instrumentation. There is no special music for small bands, medium bands and large bands; small and large bands both play or try to play the same music. In attempting to arrive at a standard international instrumentation, no traditions of existing great music could be invoked; the decisions as to what instruments were to be used, and in what proportions, could be reached only on an arbitrary basis. Moreover, since presumably each band in the world would have to make some concessions, much of the music that is now used (including the few original works of importance) would have to be rearranged.

A comparison with dance orchestra usage is in some ways as instructive as a comparison with symphony orchestra tradition. In the dance field, where the arrangement is so nearly everything, each leading dance orchestra, clinging, like the concert band, to its own instrumentation, also has its own arrangements specially made. No first-rate dance orchestra leader would dream of picking up a stock arrangement of a tune (or an arrangement made for a competitor) and using it for his group. The concert band has much in common with the dance orchestra with respect to its need for fitting the music to the instruments it includes.

It is about as difficult to speak of one arrangement being *better* than another as it is to say that Mozart's orchestration is better than Debussy's. They wrote for different orchestras, and both knew how to make an orchestra sound. A band arrangement can be judged good or bad only in relation to the band playing it; a band arrangement may look splendid on paper, but how *good* is it for a band which does not have some of the instruments for which parts are written, or for a band which perhaps has too many instruments? The instrumentation of the band may be so defective that no conceivable arrangement except one specially designed for that band's defects could sound well. The question is: Which should be blamed—the arrangement or the band?

Ideally, then, each concert band should either

have all the music it plays specially arranged for its own use or should pattern its instrumentation along the lines of some already existing band which has created a large repertory of such specially arranged music. But since the band is, especially in the United States, largely an amateur undertaking, its instrumentation is determined not so much by ideal considerations as by the practical availability of players. It thus becomes a matter of constant makeshift to approach as nearly as possible to an ideal instrumentation. The arrangements used are therefore made for that ideal instrumentation, but must take into account the variations in number and quality from the ideal. For this reason alone, it can be seen that professional and amateur bands should perhaps have entirely different arrangements; the professional band should not have to play arrangements made to provide for all possible amateur combinations, nor should the amateur band ordinarily be expected to be able to play arrangements made for the use of a specific combination of skillful professionals.

Printed band arrangements in America are now issued in conformity to a general scheme of instrumentation approved by the American Bandmasters Association and the National High School Band Association. Each arrangement issued, besides including parts for all the instruments of the *maximum* band, is designed for performance by one or two *smaller* combinations. These combinations are generally known as "Standard Band," "Concert Band" and "Symphonic Band" (the last-named for the maximum instrumentation), or whatever equivalent terms the publisher may choose. As the arranger has no means of knowing how many clarinets, cornets, tubas or saxophones will be present in any band which may play the work, his manner of writing must be cautious, to say the least. He must construct his arrangement so that a band lacking bassoons, or a second oboe, or an E*b* clarinet, can still manage to play the piece. He must, in other words, although scoring for a very large band, with theoretically "ideal" instrumentation, provide for the *absence* of any number of desirable or important instruments. He must remember, too, that while an instrument may be present, it might be risky to lean upon it too heavily. In short, he is bound to "cue in" each doubtful case: that is, he must write alternate or substitute parts to be used in case of necessity. What he *actually* does is invariably to score for the *minimum* band, building up to the maximum instrumentation by doubling various parts.

A "commercial" band arrangement of this sort is obviously limited. It can be justified as the only practical way of satisfying a large number of bands which all *strive* toward the same instrumentation, but which vary from it in large or small degree, and which range in proficiency from the highest level to the lowest. Such an arrangement is utilitarian, and is designed to withstand rough handling; it can never be considered as an absolute, but only as an expedient scheme for getting all the notes played in some shape, manner or form. The astonishing thing with these limitations is not that there are so many ill-sounding arrangements, but that there are so many which manage to be satisfactory.

It must be emphasized that, purely as a practical matter, the arranger is completely bound by his "market." Not only is his choice of instruments predetermined (he must write parts for all the instruments listed, and for no others) but to some extent even his manner of writing for them is bound by unwritten rules. The ranges of instruments are, as a rule, fairly limited, and for certain instruments parts of more than moderate difficulty must be avoided. Since most amateur bands have all their good clarinetists on the solo or first parts, it is a convention that the second and third clarinet parts must be much less difficult than the others. Another of the accepted understandings is that all players be kept as busy as possible. The reason for this in amateur bands is obvious: everyone likes to have something to do all the time. The results, musically, can be all but disastrous; if there is no musical reason for an instrument to be playing, the arranger will simply double some other part and let it go at that. His work will be judged in most cases not as an artistic accomplishment, but in terms of its complete acceptance of all the practical demands of amateur performance.

The practical differs from the ideal in a number of other respects in so far as band arrangements are concerned. The construction of band instruments in flat keys has made the use of these keys universal for all band music. Hence transposition is often necessary when a work is arranged for band from an orchestral or pianoforte original. E major will become E*b* or F; A major, either A*b* or B*b*; C♯ minor either C minor or D minor, and so on. This may be mentioned as another example of a practice to which musical purists object. It should not be necessary to add, however, that most listeners are blissfully unaware of such changes when they are made. It is probable in any case that the practice of writing entirely in flat keys will eventually disappear. Improved instruments and instrumental techniques have made performance in all keys much less difficult. Modern music, furthermore, with its shifting or multiple tonalities, makes it impossible to remain constantly in a limited range of keys; one is almost bound, in the course of any modern work, to find passages which cannot be transcribed in flat keys no matter what key has been chosen as the beginning signature.

These are a few of the practical considerations involved in present-day band arranging. There are many others which are of more specialized interest, and which are discussed from a technical standpoint in available textbooks on arranging. I have attempted here to outline the principal problems from a musical standpoint, and in a general way, in order to acquaint the reader with an essential phase of concert band performance. Many people who listen to band concerts are unaware of the thought and labor involved in preparing music so that it can be performed satisfactorily by the band. It is my belief, however, that most listeners can judge quite well whether or not a work is well arranged, and whether the effect is that of a band playing music which has been carefully prepared for it or that of a group of players struggling with music designed for some larger or smaller or differently constituted ensemble.

This effect on the listener is after all what makes a band performance acceptable or not. The happiest effect is invariably produced by a band playing music which has been arranged specifically for its own use, in which each note is played as written by the instrument specified, and in which the number of instruments has been carefully considered by the arranger. This type of arrangement is the ideal one for the concert band; it is the only sort of arrangement that can keep the band on a high artistic level and entitle it to musical respect. Most of the finest professional bands have followed this practice. The utilitarian, or universally adaptable, arrangement for the amateur band is necessary, but it cannot take the place of the arrangement designed for exact performance by a skilled ensemble with a constant instrumentation. Both types of arrangement are needed, one for serious musical purposes and the other for purely practical reasons. Neither should be neglected.

I cannot resist the temptation to reproduce, as a final note on the subject of band arrangements, an article from a Providence, Rhode Island, newspaper of 1851. This review of a concert by "The American Brass Band" (March 10, 1851) shows, if it shows nothing else, that the question was as much in the air then as now:

"The concert by the band, on Monday evening, drew, as usual, a very large audience. The instrumental performances appeared to give great satisfaction and, as we think, were in every way worthy of the high reputation which the band now enjoys. Doubtless, exceptions might be taken to some portions of the playing and to the treatment of some parts of the orchestral compositions arranged for the band, but the general effect of the full pieces was very excellent. We would remark, in this connection, that we do not acknowledge the validity of the objections made by some musical men to the reduction and arrangement, for brass instruments, of orchestral compositions. Such persons seem to us to be absurdly fastidious. Their doctrine, if generally recognized, would deprive us of the enjoyment, in any manner, of two-thirds of all the music of the greatest and best masters of the age. It would apply to all piano-forte, organ and other *arrangements* of whatever name or nature. Everybody knows, of course, that the majority of all the rich operatic overtures of the day were written for a combination of stringed, reed and wood and brass instruments, and that the genuine effects of these compositions cannot be properly realized unless they are performed by such a body of instrumentalists as they were originally composed for. Especially is this true of such an overture as Mendelssohn's 'Midsummernight's Dream,' where so much depends upon the violins and reed instruments. Our people flatter themselves that they have heard this overture, and it must be confessed that the German companies *did* give us a pretty vivid idea of it . . . nevertheless, we have *not heard the 'Midsummernight's Dream' yet.* When it shall be done here by a complete orchestra numbering some twenty-four or thirty violins, with their bows all drawn as if by the hand of one great master filled with the spirit of his author, then we shall hear it. In the meantime, let us not deprive ourselves of the elegant entertainments afforded by brass band arrangements of such fine overtures as 'Tancredi', 'Donna del Lago', 'Masaniello', 'Two Blind Men of Toledo',* and others of similar construction. That these do constitute, as played by our band, elegant, refined and elevating entertainments, no intelligent person who has heard them, we presume, will deny."

* Anyone who has attended many band concerts will recognize all of these. For those less familiar with the band repertory, the composers are, in order: Rossini, Rossini, Auber, Méhul.

CHAPTER VII

The Music of the Concert Band: Some Representative Band Programs

THE MODERN concert band has developed no significant repertory exclusively its own, but it has evolved a characteristic type of program, composed of a mixture of many sorts of music. This mixture has as its fundamental ingredient what may be called the popular classic, or standard concert favorite: music like Rossini and Mendelssohn overtures, Wagnerian excerpts, Strauss waltzes, and a general assortment of familiar nineteenth century concert pieces. To these are added selections and potpourris on tunes from the best-known grand operas, a large amount of light opera and operetta music, and movements from popular symphonies. From the military band tradition comes the march or quickstep, which is the band's greatest original contribution to its own repertory. Compositions from the pens of bandmasters, such as cornet solos, suites and characteristic pieces, are still another item. Last, but quantitatively not least, one finds a representation of familiar salon music.

The variety of band music constitutes one of its greatest charms. The band concert occupies a pleasant and necessary middle ground between the formality of the symphony concert and the tiresome doings of the salon orchestra. The band borrows music from both of these; it is the combination of the two, plus the special band pieces, that gives band concerts their uniqueness. In no other sort of concert is one likely to hear the *Egmont* Overture followed immediately by "Anchors Aweigh." Both are masterpieces of their kind; it is the juxtaposition that is startling and inimitably characteristic of band programs. The danger from the standpoint of the musically minded is, of course, that this sort of juxtaposition can be carried to a level of bad taste found otherwise only in radio revues. In most cases, however, band concerts proceed with a variety that is not only inoffensive, but often refreshing.

With the exception of a few cases where conductors and audiences have come to demand something of a musically more ambitious character, most band programs today are characterized by this variety of music, with the emphasis on the lighter side. The programs in many cases are essentially the same as they were fifty or a hundred years ago; the names of some of the composers have changed, but the type of music has not. Many of the new works are either popular pieces by fashionable composers or recently composed light music which is artistically in the same class as the greatly scorned quadrille and polka. Tastes change in the course of time, but they change more with respect to names and dates than in their essential nature.

All this is not meant to give the impression that band programs have not changed at all, or that the repertory has not been greatly extended in recent years. Programs have probably not, however, changed *in kind* as much as many people claim, despite the composition of many new works especially written for band and the exploitation of additional sources of transcribed music. The growth of a literature of original and idiomatic band music, written by serious professional composers, is perhaps the most important musical fact about bands today, and one which we shall examine separately. This literature has not yet, however, reached proportions large enough to be of major influence on band programs. Bands still rely, except for marches and a few other types of lighter music, on transcriptions from other literatures. In recent years, bandmasters have greatly enlarged their horizons so far as transcribed music is concerned. Less familiar works by the more popular masters, often neglected by the sympony orchestras, have been arranged for band, as have many compositions of early and late composers hitherto unknown to band audiences. It is today not unusual to find a band program ranging from Bach, or even Gabrieli, to Stravinsky or other important contemporaries. What still remains distinctive about such band programs is that they will in all probability include Tchaikovsky, Meyerbeer, Sousa, Verdi, Suppe and *The Carnival of Venice* en route; an assortment, in other words, nowhere else to be found in the realm of musical performance.

All this is very proper. In presenting programs of such a kind, the band is being true to its character as a medium of popular education and entertainment simultaneously. By performing serious works of a less familiar character it is making a not inconsiderable contribution of a constructive sort to what may be called popular culture. By performing new works of musical interest, especially those written exclusively for performance by bands, it is contributing to the life of music in the world. And by keeping *Poet and Peasant* and *The Carnival of Venice* alive, it is preserving a type of music which, for all that it may be played-to-death, is still dearly beloved by millions. There is something for almost anyone at an average band concert, if the music be well played.

Music that is popular is not necessarily bad. This, unfortunately, is a point of view which seems sometimes to be adopted by persons with a claim to musical sophistication. I do not mean to suggest that music which is greatly loved is necessarily good either or that one cannot get too much of anything, whether it be good or bad. I do want to suggest that it is possible to make qualitative judgments about light or popular music just as much as about serious music. There is no justification for looking down on the band, which is a popular medium, for playing light music along with more substantial fare. The band is not a competitor of the symphony orchestra. It may indeed be criticized for trying to play some of the more elaborate works from the orchestra repertory, as long as those works are still often played by the orchestra. Certainly the band cannot play them better. But the band can and should play works which, though no longer fashionable in concert halls, are still held in great affection by many people. For the à-la-mode concertgoer, some moral courage is required to admit a liking, if one exists, for music like *Poet and Peasant*. The average band audience, however, is not bothered by considerations of fashion or musical "correctness"; like Zuleika Dobson, it simply knows what it likes. The band is untrue to its character not when it plays music which its audiences want to hear, but when it tries to overreach itself and give bad imitations of other types of music.

A band's programs are, of course, determined in large part by the character of its audience. A band playing in a public park will have an audience somewhat different in nature from that attending a concert of a university band in an academic auditorium. The basic repertory is the same; the emphasis of the programming may tend toward one or another part of it. As a few examples may be illuminating, several actual programs performed by various concert bands are here set forth. These programs have been selected by the bandmasters as "typical" programs of their respective bands. All music originally written for band, that is, not transcribed, is marked with an asterisk.

The United States Navy Band, directed by Lieutenant Charles Brendler, offers programs of the following type at weekly indoor concerts during the winter months in Washington, D. C.:

Overture, "Benvenuto Cellini" ....Hector Berlioz
Wotan's Farewell and Fire Charm Music, from
"The Valkyries" ....Richard Wagner
Selection from "Natoma" ....Victor Herbert

Intermission

Invitation to the Waltz ....Weber-Weingartner
Perpetual Motion ....Nicolo Paganini
(featuring the clarinet section)
Waltz in C♯ Minor..................Fredéric Chopin
First Roumanian Rhapsody ....Georges Enesco

Another typical Navy Band program, directed by the Assistant Leader, C. W. O. Richard E. Townsend, is of interest:

Overture, "The Magic Flute" .... W. A. Mozart
Concerto in E Flat, for Trumpet .... Joseph Haydn
March to the Scaffold, from "Symphonie Fantastique" .... Hector Berlioz
Finale, Symphony in D Minor .... Cesar Franck

Intermission

A Mighty Fortress Is Our God .... Luther-Bach
Jesu, Joy of Man's Desiring .... J. S. Bach
Fugue in G Minor (The Little) .... J. S. Bach
Second Movement, Symphony No. 1 .. Howard Hanson
Guaracha, from "Latin-American Symphonette"
Morton Gould
"Stratoswing" .... Harold Walters
Siegfried's Rhine Journey, from "Goetterdaemmerung" .... Richard Wagner

The following program may be considered typical of those given by the Goldman Band on the Mall in Central Park, New York, under the direction of Edwin Franko Goldman:

*Grand March, "America"...... Edwin Franko Goldman
Suite from "The Water Music" .... G. F. Handel
An Outdoor Overture .... Aaron Copland
(arranged by the composer)
*First Suite for Band, in E*b* .... Gustav Holst
Finale from "The New World Symphony"
Antonin Dvořák

Intermission

*Festal March .... Philip James
*Fantaisie for Cornet Solo .... Del Staigers
Russian Dance from "Petrouchka"...... Igor Stravinsky
*"Lads of Wamphray" .... Percy Grainger

*March, "Anniversary" .... Edwin Franko Goldman
Waltz, "Liebeslieder" .... Johann Strauss

William D. Revelli, director of bands at the University of Michigan, gives the following as a typical program of his concert band for its appearances at the university auditorium in Ann Arbor:

Overture, "Il Matrimonio Segreto" .... Cimarosa
Prelude to Act 1, "Lohengrin" .... Wagner
*Bravada, Paso Doble .... Curzon
*Trombone Solo .... Pryor
Frühlingstimmen Waltzes .... Johann Strauss
*Rhythms of Rio .... Bennett
Capriccio Italien .... Tschaikowsky

Intermission

Three Chorals .... J. S. Bach
*March, "Varsity" .... Moore
*Mannin Veen .... Haydn Wood
*Stars and Stripes Forever .... Sousa
The Yellow and Blue (University Song)

The following program, given while the band was on tour in Canada, has been chosen as typical by Captain George S. Howard, leader of the United States Army Air Forces Band:

Overture, "Il Guarany" .... Gomez
Pavanne .... Gould
*Trombone Solo .... Pryor
Dance of the Amazons .... Liadov
Horn and Flute Duet: Serenade .... Titl
Finale from Symphony No. 4 .... Tschaikowsky

Intermission

Medley of Popular Airs
Polka from "The Golden Age" .... Shostakovitch
Russian Sailors Dance .... Glière
Saxophone Solo .... Coates
Waltz: Voices of Spring .... Strauss
Vocal Solo, "Danny Deever" .... Damrosch
Rhapsody in Blue .... Gershwin

Last, but not least significant, is a program given by the High School Band of Lenoir, North Carolina, James C. Harper, director:

Symphonic March .... Mancini
Elsa's Procession to the Cathedral, from "Lohengrin" .... Wagner
The Sorcerer's Apprentice .... Dukas
Entrance of the Bojaren .... Halvorsen
Southern Roses Waltz .... Strauss

Intermission

Il Guarany Overture .... Gomez
Ballet Suite, "La Source" .... Delibes
Tannhauser March .... Wagner
Woodwind Ensemble, "Ballet Egyptien". Luigini-Holmes
Overture to "Merry Wives of Windsor" .... Nicolai

The programs listed above are representative of those given by typical concert bands in the United States. These programs have not been dressed up or specially selected to prove any particular thesis or to show the band in a special aspect. If there are still many people who feel that bands play only cheap and secondhand music, an examination of hundreds of programs similar to those quoted should disabuse them of such feelings. Many other university bands, high school bands, and the larger service bands in the United States give programs of similar character. I believe that such programs compare favorably with those given at orchestral "pops" concerts anywhere, and in some respects have greater interest and variety.

The reader may have noted that rather few marches appear on the programs given, and may, if he is unfamiliar with band concerts, wonder what has become of that important part of the band repertory. One feature of band concerts which is not apparent on the written program is the performance of many encores or extra numbers. About half, or perhaps more, of the pieces used as encores are taken from the march repertory. It was once the practice of bandmasters to play a march or short encore selection after almost every programmed work. This practice has been pretty well abandoned, but a number of encores are invariably played at band concerts, and one is sure to hear a march or two among them.

While it is probably accurate to say that most large and proficient bands today either give programs such as those cited above or strive in that general direction, it should be noted that many amateur and school bands draw on yet another type of music. This is music written especially for amateur use, and much of it, since it is written for "educational" rather than concert purposes, lies outside the field of our study. We shall, however, have occasion to mention it again as a quantitatively important type of music composed specifically for band performance. Amateur bands also use a deplorably large number of "simplified" arrangements of many standard pieces. It is appropriate to mention these here, since there are probably one hundred or more amateur bands to every professional or semiprofessional one, and since there still exists an impression in some circles that all bands play bowdlerized versions of the so-called classics. Such versions do exist, but no good concert band today makes any use of them. The arrangements played by the leading concert bands are, with very few exceptions, direct transcriptions of the original works; they are not abbreviated or altered so as to be easier, but faithfully preserve the harmonies, rhythms, form and figurations of the originals. Unfortunately, some of the arrangements made for use by small or insufficiently proficient bands are "simplified" to the point not only of dishonesty, but of complete burlesque. Their musical and educational value is hence extremely questionable.

The esthetic and technical problems of band transcription have already been outlined, and the reader will, it is hoped, now have a reasonably clear idea of the type of transcribed music most often found on band programs. Like the orchestra, the band draws most heavily on the nineteenth century for its program material. Of all standard composers, Tchaikovsky and Wagner have probably contributed most, via transcription, to the band repertory. Their music, long since popularized by orchestras everywhere, lends itself singularly well to band instrumentation. (In passing, one might remark on the amount of Wagner played at the Paris Festival in 1867; even then, when the music was comparatively new, it was recognized as admirable material for the wind band.) Music of a "dramatic" character has always held a leading place on band programs. Meyerbeer is no longer fashionable, but his music was once a staple of the band repertory; Verdi, too, was at one time one of the composers most frequently represented at concerts in parks and public places. That their places have been taken by Tchaikovsky and Wagner is more a matter of change of names and fashions than of fundamental musical character.

There is possibly less operatic music on concert band programs today than there was a generation ago. But the standard overtures and concert pieces are the same in kind as ever. The principal change has been the growth of popular interest (and as a consequence of interest on the part of bandmasters) in the music of Bach, which is a matter of the past twenty years or less. Transcriptions of Bach's music for orchestra preceded and made possible the band versions of the same works. So far as transcriptions are concerned, the band plays it safe: it adopts for its own repertory only works by recognized "masters," or works of established popularity. Contemporary works as a rule are transcribed only when they have become familiar as part of the orchestral repertory. As band concerts reflect, as well as help to guide, popular taste, this conservative attitude toward the repertory is perfectly natural.

Interest in the transcription of contemporary music for band is certainly not greater today than it was in 1867, when Wagner, Rossini, Ambroise Thomas and Gounod, all of whom were then alive and flourishing, were handsomely represented at the great band festival in Paris. Such interest is today about the same as it was then, or is perhaps even a trifle less. The great difference today is in the cultivation of an *original* and serious literature for band, not transcribed at all. In performing serious new works not previously made popular by the orchestra, the band can be a pioneering agency. So important is the development of this repertory, and so great is its potentiality for giving the band a musical mission of greater scope than it has ever had before, that it must be considered as an entirely separate subject.

CHAPTER VIII

Original Music for Band. Band Scores

THE MUSIC played by the early town and military bands of Europe is not, of course, band music in the modern sense. It belongs to the band tradition, since these small groups were the precursors of the concert band, but the music they played (such of it as is preserved) appears to us today in the light of ensemble music, which must be transcribed for modern band performance just as much as any other music, not written for wind instruments, of the same period. It is on the whole neither more nor less appropriate for transcription than the string music or vocal music of preclassical times. There are a few exceptional instances, mostly among the music for brasses, a good approximation of which can be given today by the brass players of a concert band. The four- and five-part pieces of Pezel (fl. 1670) or Reiche (1667-1734) can be played by brasses in any multiple of four or five making up a true choir. This is still, needless to say, not band music in the ordinary sense. The sonate and canzone of Giovanni Gabrieli have already been mentioned; these magnificent works can be played with inspiring sonority by modern brasses. Some have recently been revived, but they have not become generally known, and it cannot be said that they have been included, as they should be, in the repertory of today's concert band.

The music written by Lully for the oboe bands of the seventeenth century French army is simple four-part music which, unlike the brass music, would have to be filled out and elaborated for modern wind band performance, and as the pieces are themselves neither full nor elaborate their character would be entirely distorted by such a procedure and they would have little relation to the original except historical derivation and association. There might, of course, be some point in reviving these works, for a special festival or educational project, in as nearly original form as possible (that is, on modern double reeds), to show some of the ancestry of contemporary band music. Otherwise they are of no interest to the modern band.

In another volume I have cited and discussed the original band works of the eighteenth and nineteenth centuries, music which is full of historical interest, but which remains unknown to all except a few specialists. Here I shall review briefly some of the more interesting works, in the hope that by thus calling attention to them again I may help to stimulate a revival of interest in them on the part of bandsmen and other musicians. It is true that the eighteenth century marches and other "band" works cannot be played in anything approaching their original form by modern bands, but some of them have a definite educational and musical value as wind ensemble music, in which form they should be performed if they are to be performed at all. Handel, Haydn, J. C. Bach, Mozart, Shield, Dibdin, Reinagle, K. P. E. Bach and a number of other rather famous composers wrote music which was in its time "band" music. The music played by the 2 oboes, 2 clarinets, 2 horns and 2 bassoons in the second act of Mozart's *Don Giovanni* is actually meant to represent a band concert, the instrumentation and character of the music (a pot-pourri on operatic airs) being completely characteristic of the period. Haydn wrote a number of little occasional pieces for bands. Rather recently I learned of two marches which had hitherto escaped my attention. The music is entitled: "Two Marches, Composed by J. Haydn, M. D., for Sir Henry Harper, Bart., and presented by him to the Volunteer Cavalry of Derbyshire. Embodied in the year 1794." * J. C. Bach also wrote a few marches for English military bands, and it is said that the march in *Scipio* was first written by Handel as a parade march for the Grena-

* In the Free Library of Philadelphia, Fleisher Collection. Scored for 2 clarinets, 2 bassoons, serpent, 2 horns, and trumpets.

A sample "condensed" band score. Copyright, 1941, by Music Press Incorporated. Reprinted here by permission of the copyright owner.

dier Guards. Frederick the Great was an enthusiastic bandsman, and wrote at least one march for military band. K. P. E. Bach was perhaps the most prolific band composer of the century; it is a misfortune that most of the works he wrote for small eighteenth century bands, including four symphonies, appear to be lost.

The works written in France at the time of the Revolution are the first that begin to meet our conception of band music in size and character. Modern bands can perform many of these compositions, with reasonable adaptation for modern instruments, without changing their essential character. Perhaps the revolutionary origin of these works has operated against them in the eyes of military bandmasters, although it is difficult to define what precisely is "revolutionary" about a work unadornedly entitled *Symphony for Wind Instruments* or *Overture for Military Band.* They have, for whatever reason, fallen into undeserved neglect, and a resurrection of some of these pieces, notably the overture written by Méhul and the two symphonies of Gossec, would appear to be of great interest not only to band amateurs but to musicians everywhere. The Méhul overture is scored for 2 piccolos, 1st and 2nd clarinets, 2 trumpets, 2 horns in F, 2 bassoons, serpent, bass trombone, and timpani. It was in all probability performed by the band of the National Guard which, in the year the

Overture was written, consisted of 54 players. A larger instrumentation is indicated in one of the overtures of Catel, scored for 2 flutes, 2 piccolos, 1st and 2nd clarinets, 2 horns, 2 trumpets, 2 bassoons, 3 trombones, serpent, and timpani. Besides the already mentioned symphonies of Gossec, there are a number of marches by the same composer, and several dignified hymns, written for open-air performance by large chorus with wind band accompaniment. Of Catel, there are two symphonies, two overtures and a number of marches, many of which are still of musical interest. Lesueur, the teacher of Berlioz, Jadin, Soler, Ozi, and nearly every other French composer of note at that time wrote some pieces for wind band.

It cannot be said that the composers of the nineteenth century wrote extensively for band, although there are more band works by celebrated composers than one would suspect from a review of band programs or from most writings on the subject. Beethoven's marches and Weber's small pieces are fairly negligible from a musical standpoint, although interesting historically as minor works of major figures. Beethoven wrote four marches, a polonaise and an écossaise; Weber, a march, a waltz and a number of fanfares. Spontini, Meyerbeer, Spohr and Rossini, as well as Paër, Pleyel, Paisiello and Cherubini, all wrote marches for military bands. An especially melancholy flavor was introduced into band music when it became customary to use bands at funerals. Donizetti, Ponchielli, Schubert, Grieg and Wagner each enriched the band repertory with one or more funeral marches, and Berlioz wrote his huge *Funeral and Triumphal Symphony* for wind band. This amazing work, almost without a doubt the greatest ever written for wind band, deserves a chapter by itself. It was written for the tenth anniversary of the Revolution of July, 1830, and was first performed in Paris on July 28, 1840. Wagner wrote of this work that it finally convinced him of the greatness of Berlioz. The full title of the work as given on the title page of the original edition, is: "Grand Funeral and Triumphal Symphony, for large military band, with string orchestra and chorus *ad libitum,* composed for the consolation of the remains of the victims of July, and for the inauguration of the Bastille Column, and dedicated to His Royal Highness, Monseigneur the Duke of Orleans, by Hector Berlioz." The symphony is in three parts: Funeral March, Prayer, and Apotheosis, and the score calls for 108 players, with a string orchestra of 80 and a chorus of 200 (in the last movement only) *ad libitum.* As the work has never, to my knowledge, been performed in the United States, and since it is known to most musicians only as a vague reference, I believe the scoring, which I reproduce in the order given by Berlioz, will be of great interest:

1 piccolo in D*b*
5 flutes in E*b*
5 clarinets in E*b*
14 1st clarinets in B*b*
12 2nd clarinets in B*b*
5 oboes

12 horns, in F, A*b* and C (divided in 6 parts)
8 trumpets, in F and C (divided in 4 parts)
4 cornets-à-pistons in A*b* (divided in 2 parts)

4 1st trombones (altos or tenors)
3 2nd trombones (tenors)
3 3rd trombones (tenors)
1 bass trombone (*ad lib*)
3 ophicleides in C
3 ophicleides in B*b*

2 bass clarinets in B*b*
8 bassoons (1st and 2nd)
1 contra bassoon (*ad lib*)

20 1st violins (*ad lib*)
20 2nd violins (*ad lib*)
15 violas (*ad lib*)
15 violoncellos (*ad lib*)
10 string basses (*ad lib*)

14 percussion players

The 'cellos and string basses are included in the score in all three movements; the violas and violins are added in the final movement only. The second movement features a long recitative and solo for the tenor trombone, and the following note is included in the score: "If there is no tenor trombone player skillful enough to perform the solo part of this piece, it may be played on an alto valve trombone in F, or on a horn in G (with valves), or on a bass clarinet in C. The solo is arranged by the composer for each of these three instruments, and parts are available." We see how early composers found it necessary to cue parts in band compositions.

It is futile to attempt a description of this work, and it is to be hoped that bands will one day let it be heard again.* No work of comparable grandeur has ever been written for wind band. It is interesting to note that Berlioz himself directed performances of the symphony in Germany and in Russia as well as in France.

Other nineteenth century band works appear quite trivial when mentioned after the Berlioz symphony. Spohr wrote an interesting *Nocturne in C* and Mendelssohn wrote a charming overture in the same key, known as the *Military Overture,* Opus 24. This was written in 1824 for the band at the resort of Dobberan on the Baltic Sea, where the young composer, then all of fifteen years old,† was summering with his family. The original instrumentation was small but rather complete, and is interesting for its inclusion

* My edition of this symphony, a faithful adaptation for modern band of the original score, will be available in 1947.

† When I mentioned the date of this work to a noted musicologist, he commented: "Ah, yes, of course—that was Mendelssohn's best period!"

of parts for basset horn in F. Even in Mendelssohn's day, Wieprecht rearranged it for larger band. It is a thoroughly characteristic Mendelssohn overture and has been played more or less consistently in adaptations for modern instruments. It was revived by the Goldman Band during the 1945 season in New York. Sir George Grove, in his famous article on Mendelssohn in *Grove's Dictionary,* states that among Mendelssohn's works of 1826 is "an interesting-looking *Andante and Allegro* (June 27), written for the wind band of a Beer-garden which he used to pass on his way to bathe." The manuscript of this piece has probably been lost.

Wagner composed two band works: the *Weber Funeral March* (*Trauermarsch zur Beisetzung C.M. von Webers*) and a *Homage March* (*Huldigungsmarsch*), neither of which is often played today. The Weber piece was composed in 1844 for the ceremonies attendant on the transference of Weber's remains to Dresden, and is based on two themes from *Euryanthe.* The score is comparatively modest, calling for only 75 players plus six muffled side drums. The instrumentation is for 5 flutes, 4 first oboes, 3 second oboes, 20 B*b* clarinets (five players on each of four parts), 5 first and 5 second bassoons, 4 first and 4 second horns, 6 trumpets in F, 3 first and 3 second B*b* tenor horns, 3 alto, 3 tenor and 3 bass trombones, 4 tubas in C, and the drums. The score remained in manuscript until 1926, when it was published in Germany. The *Huldigungsmarsch* has never been published in its original form. It was written in 1864 for King Ludwig II of Bavaria and was scored for performance by military band. Wagner began to score the work for orchestra, but turned it over to Joachim Raff for completion. Versions played by bands today are transcribed from Raff's orchestral score.

It is probable that many of the Russian composers wrote band works toward the end of the century, but few of such works are extant. Tchaikovsky wrote a slight but competent Military March in 1892, and Rimsky-Korsakov wrote a set of *Variations on a Theme of Glinka,* as well as concertos for clarinet and trumpet (or trombone) with band accompaniment. None of these works is particularly remarkable; their existence should, however, be known to bandsmen and musicians who believe that no one ever wrote anything for band prior to the contemporary efforts in that direction.

Efforts have occasionally been made in the past to interest composers in writing for wind band. Contests have been held, and inducements offered composers to write music for special occasions. One such contest was held in England in 1872, with Sir Arthur Sullivan presiding over the committee of judges. Nothing of great interest has ever come of these attempts, and I mention them only to show that the problem of creating an original repertory has always been present in the minds of serious bandsmen.

The twentieth century brought with it a strong revival of interest in idiomatic writing for wind instruments, reflected not only in the composition of a great many works for small wind ensembles but in the general style of orchestral writing. The interest has not yet extended on a vast scale to composition for bands, but a number of very substantial works have been written, and there is every reason to believe that interest in the wind band is growing. Prior to the 1930's, few important band works appeared; the emergence of a real movement to enlarge the band's literature of original music has come about only in the past two decades or less. Gustav Holst's *First Suite for Band,* in E*b,* written in 1909, and his *Second Suite,* in F, written in about 1911, are the first twentieth century band works of any consequence with which we have to deal. Holst was a capable trombonist, and had considerable experience with bands, facts which show clearly in the skill with which he handled the band medium. The music of the suites is typical of Holst at his best; it is direct, and yet sensitive, and shows the deep influence of English folk song. The *Second Suite* is, in fact, based on country tunes, the last movement being identical with the final movement of the *Saint Paul's Suite* for string orchestra. A comparison of these two versions is recommended to all students interested in learning to write for band, as Holst's reworking of the music in the *Second Band Suite* can teach more than a dozen textbooks on arranging. A third band work by Holst, the Prelude and Scherzo, *Hammersmith,* was written in about 1930, but has never been published. Only the *First Suite* has been published in full score, and this version has been altered by the addition of fluegelhorns and other instruments to suit the requirements of American high school "contest" rules.

Two splendid compositions for band by Ralph Vaughan Williams appeared in 1924. They are an *English Folk-Song Suite,* in three movements, and a *Toccata Marziale.* The latter is a solid and vigorous work exceptionally suited in character to the wind band medium and brilliantly scored to exhibit its possibilities. The *Folk-Song Suite* must inevitably be compared to Holst's *Second Suite,* which in general feeling it resembles. It is the first modern example (the Wagner *Huldigungsmarsch* is the only earlier one) of which I know of a band original being later transcribed for orchestra,* reversing the time-honored procedure.

The Holst and Vaughan Williams works illustrate the point made in an earlier chapter with regard to the national character of most band works,

* By Gordon Jacob.

including those by serious composers. Although these are not patriotic anthems or marches, the national character is given by the folk idiom employed. Many of Percy Grainger's works for band are of the same tendency, even where actual folk melodies are not employed. Grainger became interested in composing for band during World War I, when he was a bandsman in the United States army, and has since written a large number of original band works, in addition to making band arrangements of many of his famous folk settings. Grainger's scoring for band has a rich sonority and color which compares favorably with any celebrated example of brilliant orchestration. His setting of the *Irish Tune from County Derry* has a sheer beauty of sound which should make any listener love the band. In his later works for band, such as the *Lincolnshire Posy* (1937) and *Lads of Wamphray* (1938), the scoring is more daring and original. These works are difficult, requiring a band of skillful players and above all a musicianly and expert conductor, but one must hear them (as well as the suites of Williams and Holst) played by a good band, not cluttered up with extra instruments or overweighted with any group or groups of instruments, to appreciate what a splendid medium the wind band can be.

About 1930, works for band by composers of international reputation began to become more numerous. Respighi, Roussel, Florent Schmitt, Toch,

Hindemith, Křenek, Weinberger, Prokofiev and Miaskovsky are among the European composers who wrote one or more compositions for wind band during the thirties. It is evident that these are composers of diverse schools; the works are of course of unequal importance and quality. The band works of Prokofiev and Křenek are marches, but rather interesting and original ones. Miaskovsky has written not only a march, but a symphony (his nineteenth) as well. Florent Schmitt wrote two works, both of great difficulty, for the band of the Garde Républicaine; the works of Respighi and Roussel were written for American bands, and are scored accordingly. All of Weinberger's band works, of which there are several, were written after the composer settled in the United States, and were designed for American instrumentation. We have already discussed the impediment to international circulation of band works caused by the differences in instrumentation of various countries. Although the band works of Roussel, Respighi and Weinberger have received frequent performances in the United States, I am not in a position to state whether or not they have had much circulation abroad. The Russian works are played by American bands in adapted versions, with added saxophones and other parts lacking in the original scores.

These works need not detain us, since in nearly every case they are minor efforts of well-known men.

The scoring is seldom of exceptional interest, except for the fact that it *is* scoring for wind band directly. One feels in some cases, however, the unfamiliarity of the composers with the idiom. Respighi's *Huntingtower Ballad,* written in 1932, is a short somber work with some interesting exploitation of the lower wind instruments. It is a good repertory piece, but it will never compete in popular affection with the composer's *Pines of Rome,* played by bands in transcription. (One New York reviewer observed that it sounded much better in band transcription than it did in the original!) Florent Schmitt's *Dionysiaques* (1925) is perhaps the most ambitious of the works mentioned above, and is notable for its brilliant writing. Prokofiev's *Athletic Festival March* (1935) is extremely jolly, an ideal sort of music for a popular event.

In more recent years, since 1940, writing for band has assumed the proportions of a real movement, especially in the United States. Among the composers who have written wind band compositions in this country are native composers and Europeans now resident here, including Arnold Schoenberg, Igor Stravinsky, Darius Milhaud, Pedro Sanjuan, Henry Cowell, Roy Harris, Paul Creston, Wallingford Riegger, William Schuman, Gail Kubik, Leo Sowerby, Samuel Barber, William Grant Still, Daniel Gregory Mason, Arthur Shepherd, Morton Gould, Philip

James, Robert Russell Bennett, Burnet Tuthill, George F. McKay, Henry Hadley, John Alden Carpenter, Bainbridge Crist, Ray Green, Dai-Keong Lee, James R. Gillette, Herbert Haufrecht, Joseph Wagner, Normand Lockwood, Arthur Kreutz, Robert McBride, Robert Sanders, and a number of others. This activity continues, as it does in other countries, where John Ireland, Shostakovich, Glière and Khachaturian, among others, have recently added works to the band repertory. Many of the leading composers of South and Central America have written works for band.

It is not my intention to represent this music as more than it is—a hopeful beginning of a new day for band music—or to pretend that many of the new band works are of the highest musical interest. It is always difficult to evaluate the enduring qualities of any contemporary music, and doubly so in the case of *Gebrauchsmusik,* or music written for generally practical and utilitarian ends. Many of the new pieces (those of Shostakovich and Barber, for example) are military marches, brought up to date. Others are typically light or even humorous compositions. (The Stravinsky band work is his since much-transcribed *Circus Polka,* written originally for a circus band.)

What is important for the future of bands, and for the enlargement of everyone's musical horizon, is that interest in the band as a medium has spread to a large number of composers, representing many schools of esthetics, that among these composers are to be found many of the younger composers of talent or promise, and that among the many pieces written are some few of really serious intent and skillful execution. It is true that there are no symphonies among these works, but it is also true that too many people take length and pretentiousness as their only criteria of importance and seriousness. (One might note that a great deal of pompous garbage is written, for band and otherwise, called "symphonic," or "grand," or bearing some other type of inflated description, to foster some baseless illusion in the mind of the composer or the audience or both. It is a great misfortune for our youngsters that so much "educational" music falls into this category.) Most of the new band works of the composers named can stand on their own merits if they are taken for what they are: music written for a certain combination of instruments, to be played for a mass audience wanting to be entertained. Within that sphere, they may justly be considered "major" works.

A few of them qualify as interesting and substantial creations by any standard. Schoenberg's extraordinary *Theme and Variations for Wind Band,* Opus 43a, written in 1943, is nothing if not highly serious, undoubtedly too much so for most band audiences. An extremely complex work, rich in invention and rewarding in the quality of its ideas, it represents a landmark in the history of band literature. The only performances of the work (at this writing) in its original form have been those given by the Goldman Band under the author's direction. An orchestral transcription of the work was presented by the Boston Symphony, under Koussevitsky, and later by the New York Philharmonic under Stokowski.

Milhaud also transcribed his *Suite Française* (1945) for orchestra, but after it had been played in its original form by the Goldman Band and others. The Milhaud suite is thoroughly ingratiating, in the folk idiom like the Holst and Vaughan Williams suites, but spiced with more advanced and piquant sounds. It is scored with great brilliance and assurance, full of contrast in its five movements, and says what it has to say with economy and taste. This work may well be recommended for study. Milhaud's *Two Marches* (1945) give further proof of his mastery of the band idiom and a suitably "popular" style.

Henry Cowell's *Shoonthree* (1941), a work of great beauty and expressiveness, also was scored for orchestra by the composer after it had been often performed in its original form by wind bands, and a comparison of the scores is interesting. Cowell has written a number of works for band, most of them in a simple idiom suitable for school use. In *Shoonthree* and in the *Celtic Set* (1939), Cowell has tellingly ex-

First page of composer's autograph score of *Suite Française* by Darius Milhaud, showing layout and number of parts. Copyright, 1945, by Leeds Music Corporation, New York, N. Y. Reprinted here by permission of the copyright owner.

ploited the tonal resources of the band, and the scores are models of skill and ingenuity in contrasting the colors of wind instruments.

Many of the other new works are noteworthy. The *Canto Yorubà* of Pedro Sanjuan (1942), a large work in Afro-Cuban style, is a sensationally vigorous and compelling piece, with fine rhythmic drive and genuine mastery in band scoring. Sanjuan, like Holst and Grainger, learned about the wind band at first hand, thereby no doubt acquiring the sureness of touch which characterizes the *Canto Yorubà* and his two more recent band works. These pieces have authenticity in addition to quality, in grateful contrast to the synthetic "Cuban" and "Latin" music with which we have been so mercilessly afflicted. Certainly the *Canto Yorubà* is unique in the band repertory. Paul Creston's *Legend* (1942) is in all respects more conventional, but is striking in its warmth and flow. It, too, is splendidly scored, with special skill shown in the handling of saxophones, horns and baritone. Wallingford Riegger's *Prelude and Fugue* (1943) represents still another type of music found among the new works for band. It is a serious work of a fine musician, full of ingenious ideas, and very successfully cast in the band's instrumental idiom.

The compositions mentioned may give the reader a small idea of the work being done today in the field of original music for bands. Among the other works are overtures and concert pieces of varying interest. Many of them are pioneering efforts, in that they open up new musical values in wind band performance, while others are of more conventional content and treatment. Some give the impression of tentativeness in dealing with the band as a medium (a difficulty which will right itself when a *tradition* of band composition has been achieved) ; others are satisfactory except that they indefinably sound like transcriptions of works written for orchestra. One should mention here several works of interest which, although written for orchestra, have been transcribed for band by their composers. Notable among these is the *Outdoor Overture* of Aaron Copland, which in the author's opinion, is even brighter and more vigorous in the band version than in the original. This overture makes band music of the most suitable sort, but the band version, unfortunately, remains in manuscript at this writing. Another similarly successful transcription was made by Riegger of the Finale of his *New Dance,* an extraordinarily vital and exciting composition full of alarming but stimulating rhythmic complexities.

Besides these works by composers who have established reputations in the orchestral field, there are many compositions of merit by men who have specialized in the band field and who are known primarily as bandmasters or arrangers. Among them are Erik

W. G. Leidzén, Charles O'Neill, Peter Buys, and several others, who write straightforward and knowingly scored works which please audiences and players alike. Pleasing the players is an especially important consideration in band music, it may be noted, since nearly all the organizations are composed of amateurs. While most music of this type is "practical" music designed to answer the needs of school and amateur bands, there is no reason why such music should not be substantial and honest. Although an immense amount of utter trash is written in this category, it is a pleasure to be able to note that some of the musicians who write for the schools can combine practicality with taste and sound musicianship.

Of marches I think I need hardly speak. I would scarcely be doing justice to the American reader if I did not assume him to be familiar with Bagley's *National Emblem,* Zimmerman's *Anchors Aweigh,* Reeves's *2nd Connecticut Regiment,* Bigelow's *Our Director,* Goldman's *On the Mall* and a large selection of the works of Sousa. Each generation produces new marches to stand with the past's masterpieces in this genre. They form, as has been said before, the unique and indispensable part of the band repertory, and there are classics among them. Sousa was to the march what Strauss was to the waltz; and the march is to the band what the waltz is to the salon orchestra. Each nation, moreover, has its own treasury of traditional and favorite marches, and its own special genius for turning out marches according to the national taste.

Band Scores

When a composer writes a work for an instrumental ensemble, whether it be chamber group, orchestra or band, he writes each instrumental part on a separate line, so that the notes assigned to each instrument are clearly differentiated and independent. In a band score there will usually be about thirty such separate lines. The reader will find a page of full band score reproduced in this volume to show the appearance of such a score and the order in which the instruments are generally placed. A full score of this sort is not only an essential part of the process of composition, but it is indispensable to the conductor who is to study and perform the work. All works for symphony orchestra are made available in full score to conductors; most band works, for reasons which we shall discuss, are made available only in reduced or condensed scores, in which all the notes originally written on twenty to thirty lines are compressed into three or four lines, with indications of the division of instrumental parts. Often band scores are reduced to two-line piano arrangements, and not very long ago it was not uncommon to find that the only part available to the conductor was a melody part (generally cornet or clarinet) with the "accompaniment" lightly indicated.

It is obvious that a conductor cannot be expected to give an understanding performance of a work if he does not know what notes each instrument is supposed to play and if he does not clearly perceive the relation of the parts to the whole. Such knowledge can be derived only from a complete score which shows him exactly what the composer or arranger has written. A well-made condensed score can often be adequate, if the instrumental cues are clearly indicated and if the conductor takes the trouble to supplement his study of the conductor's score by an examination of the individual parts. But this is a roundabout and clumsy way of doing things, involving a considerable waste of time. The conductor, of whom we shall have more to say in the next chapter, should come to the first reading or rehearsal of a new work with the music well in mind. With bands, the conductor often can learn a piece of music only as he hears it played, because there is no detailed score which he can study in advance. He can of course learn the outlines and in many cases even the essentials of a work from his condensed score, but he cannot learn the details unless he examines each instrumental part or until he commences his rehearsals.

At one time, it was perhaps not necessary that complete band scores be made available. When the

SHOONTHREE

HENRY COWELL

Conductor's "condensed" score, on four and three staves, of an original band work. Copyright, 1943, by Mercury Music Corporation, New York, N. Y. Reprinted here by permission of the copyright owner.

band's repertory consisted of nothing but very familiar items, the conductor could be expected to have heard them so many times as to know them all by rote. He could almost always make a correct guess as to which instrument would, or should, be playing when, because of his familiarity with routine band arranging. He would furthermore not be able to use a large score even if it were available, for the chances are that he would be playing out of doors, where the problem of turning pages and keeping the music from blowing away is often beyond solution. He would conduct most pieces from memory, or use what amounts to a shorthand score as a guide.

With new works for band, of a completely unstereotyped character, it is no longer possible to make shift in this manner. The conductor can no longer guess at the correct harmony, voice movement or instrumentation. Ideally, full scores should be made available for all important band works. Failing that, the condensed scores (of which examples are reproduced) must be made as complete as possible. In recent years, condensed scores have become much more detailed and satisfactory, but they are still only a substitute for full scores. The resistance to using full scores, which is encountered occasionally among bandmasters, will disappear as the repertory of important new works grows, and as bandmasters come to realize that it is often easier to read a full score than a condensed one. The importance of the score is primarily for rehearsal and study. Working with a band which has practically unlimited time to prepare for an occasional concert, a bandmaster can afford to take the necessary time during rehearsal to find out, if necessary, just what is written for each instrument. With any band having to prepare a good deal of music in a limited time, such a procedure is impossible. In performance, of course, it does not matter what the conductor uses, provided he knows the music thoroughly. Many conductors prefer to perform from memory, but if they are good conductors one may be sure that they have first learned every note of the music through study and rehearsal.

For students, the full score is a necessity, although the energetic student can of course reconstruct the full score from the condensed score and the individual parts. With many band works fully worthy of serious study, a demand should be created for the publication of complete band scores similar to those made available for orchestral works. Some of the important new band works have appeared in full score, as have a number of band arrangements in recent years. No other phenomenon connected with band music today gives a better indication of the increasing importance and seriousness of the concert band or offers more encouragement for its future development.

CHAPTER IX

The Bandmaster. Seating and Tuning the Band Outdoor Concerts

THE BANDMASTER and the conductor of an orchestra do much the same thing: they set the tempo of the music, beat time, exercise the privilege of "interpreting" musical works, choose the programs they wish to play, hire and fire the members of the ensemble, cajole or threaten the players into carrying out their wishes, and are in general responsible for the artistic and popular success of their organizations. Artistically, the bandmaster has very much the same problems to meet as the conductor of "popular" orchestral concerts. In both cases, entertainment is the primary object, and the programs must be constructed to suit all tastes. The bandmaster must have a good sense of his audience's reactions, and must have "audience appeal" of a different type from that of the symphony conductor. The bandmaster has perhaps more of a responsibility than most other conductors in guiding the tastes of his listeners while entertaining them, for the band is by tradition a popular medium, and the first acquaintance of many people with music is, or used to be, through the band. Since the bandmaster must give his audience very varied fare, ranging from cornet solos and light opera potpourris to serious overtures and symphonic pieces, it is necessary that he have an extremely catholic knowledge of, and familiarity with, all types of music. Most important, if he is good at his job, he must have a knowledge of *style,* embracing all these types of music; he must know how to play a march or a symphony or a bit of lightweight fluff with a real understanding of the music's character. I am afraid that many people have heard bands playing Beethoven overtures as if they were military marches, and bits of nothings as if they were melodramatic operas. The competent bandmaster must have rather universal adaptability. To have that, he should have a solid grounding in a variety of music *other* than band music.

Most of the work of the bandmaster or orchestra conductor is done at rehearsals, before the public performance becomes possible. Here, too, the work of the bandmaster parallels that of any other director. It is at rehearsals that the ensemble of an organization is created, for no matter how excellent the individual players, they must become co-ordinated and routined to playing as one instrument responsive to the leader. It is not only precision in playing together that the conductor must exact from the players, but tonal balance and blending. The amount accomplished at a rehearsal depends on the sureness of the conductor in knowing what he wants and how to achieve it. A conductor's rehearsal technique can be his greatest asset, for as a rule rehearsal time is limited for both professional and amateur bands, and it is necessary to accomplish as much as possible in the time available. We have already noted the amount of time that may be wasted in rehearsal by reason of the lack of full scores for many band works. The bandmaster should have a good idea of a new work from study of a "condensed" score, but it is understandable and excusable if he is not completely enlightened concerning a few precise details. This means time lost in rehearsal, and any such lost time, since it must be made up in the rehearsal of that work or another, necessarily shows in the band's public performance.

The principal difference between the bandmaster and the orchestra conductor resides in the fact that the instrumentation the latter may use is clearly indicated in his scores, while the bandmaster may decide *a priori* on any instrumentation he likes, to do duty for every type of music his band will play. The orchestra conductor has no discretionary powers (or should have none) to enlarge Beethoven's orchestra or to decide that he will use saxophones instead of bassoons; he should be no more than a faithful execu-

The Goldman Band, Edwin Franko Goldman, conductor, San Francisco, 1939.

The University of Michigan Concert Band, William D. Revelli, conductor.

tant of the composer's expressed design. The bandmaster, for reasons which have been pointed out, has no such guide or tradition; he has therefore an additional responsibility: that of choosing what seems to him the best combination of instruments consistent with the available arrangements and original compositions and with his choice of repertory. This is a much more serious responsibility than is generally recognized. The conductor of an orchestra will as a general thing not try to perform a work calling for more instrumental resources than those which he has at his disposal, nor will he perform Haydn symphonies with a full battery of instruments Haydn never employed. There are bandmasters, however, who expect each work to fit their own instrumentation (whether it be 30 or 100 players), and who, if the work necessitates a larger, smaller or merely different combination, are not unwilling to place the blame on the composer or arranger.

The ideal bandmaster should himself be a competent band arranger. It is his responsibility to see that the music he chooses be played as well as possible and that his combination of instruments be used to the best possible advantage. No printed arrangement or composition for band can, even under relatively standardized patterns, possibly be completely satisfactory for each and every different band, and the bandmaster will in many cases have to make minor changes and adaptations not only for the instruments he has but, in the case of amateur bands, for the capacities of individual players as well. The extent to which such adaptation is artistically permissible in the case of works written for band is, of course, an open question. Most realistic composers are aware of the problems involved in the variation of band combinations and try to write their scores so as to provide for as many contingencies as possible, leaving the best resolution of some of the problems directly to the discretion of the bandmaster.

A variation of this problem is presented by the fact that there are often many arrangements or editions available of a given work from the standard repertory. This embarrassment of choice never faces the orchestra conductor; there is only one version of a standard symphony or of any music he is likely to play. The bandmaster is often faced with an appalling amount of choice in the matter of arrangements, and only if he himself is somewhat skilled in the matter of arranging will he be able to decide which arrangement is best. There are, for example, at least seven band arrangements of Suppe's *Light Cavalry* Overture published in America, besides innumerable foreign editions; there are six or more domestic band arrangements of "The Beautiful Blue Danube" offered for sale, and similarly large numbers of all the other war horses of the repertory. They are not all equally good, or equally bad, as the case may be; there is a great variety of crime that can be concealed under the heading "arrangement," and the bandmaster can weed out the good from the bad only if he is technically equipped to deal with the matter. Many of the arrangements unfortunately deviate in important respects (harmony, rhythm, and so on) from the originals; in order to evaluate the arrangement, it is therefore also necessary that the bandmaster be familiar with the original of the work. Poor arrangements can of course not be made to sound well no matter how fine the band may be. No really good bandmaster will ever permit himself to perform a work in any but an arrangement which he knows to be satisfactory.

Familiarity with all the instruments is of course necessary for the bandmaster, who should be able to play one or more of them. It is advantageous if he is a pianist as well, since it is often useful, in studying new works, to read them at the piano with the full harmonies. That, however, is less important than experience in playing a wind or stringed instrument in a band or orchestra under a first-rate conductor. Conducting cannot be taught like arithmetic; it must be learned through practice and experience, and there is no better way of learning than through the practical method of studying at first hand the technique and methods of a fine conductor. Many of the ablest conductors have served apprenticeships as orchestral players; as such they became familiar with the meaning of the baton and with more or less authoritative readings of works in the standard repertory. Playing in a good orchestra or band serves also to develop the ear to detect falsities of intonation or execution, and it is needless to point out that the conductor must have a fine ear as one of his first qualifications.

The technique of the baton is itself fairly simple, and can easily be learned. Using the baton gracefully and expressively, however, cannot be taught at all, but must be a natural gift. The conductor's (or bandmaster's) gestures not only serve to beat time; they command the players in every aspect of nuance, volume, phrasing and timing. The best conductor is not necessarily the one who is most acrobatic, or who conducts with his feet or his hair, but the one who is so firmly in command that he obtains the respect and obedience of the players, and whose gestures and use of the baton are always meaningful to the players instead of to the gallery.

One should not minimize the gallery, however; a conductor's popular success usually depends on it, and many a conductor has made his way in the world on nothing much more than a good figure, a good tailor, and an air of being a genius. If a conductor knows what he is doing, his mannerisms are comparatively unimportant. An awareness of the audience and its reactions is an essential part of showmanship, which is in turn something the conductor or bandmaster must understand. Bandmasters generally appreciate the need for showmanship, and rightly so, for they deal as a rule with audiences who understand and appreciate it in its simplest forms. The uniforming of bands is an elementary aspect of the matter, as is the ramrod stiffness often favored by bandmasters trained in the military tradition. This rigidness is of course pure and simple showmanship; it may work very well, and present a crisp appearance when beating time for a march, but it is somewhat limiting, as well as incongruous, on occasions when another sort of expressiveness may be desirable. This type of band-leading technique—feet firmly together, back stiff, shoulders rigid, arm moved only from the elbow—is unquestionably a hangover from a day when a military bandmaster was supposed to be not so much a musician as a soldier whose duty it was to beat time. Gold braid and medals do not make a musician, though they often used to make a bandmaster.

Extremes in either direction are about equally distressing, although many of them make good reading. John Tasker Howard, in his book *Our American Music,* has a vivid account of the conducting of Louis Antoine Jullien, a man whose extravagant antics on and off the stage set a model which has often since been imitated but never surpassed. There have been bandmasters whose ideas of showmanship were of the Jullien school, who climbed up a few steps when the band played louder and climbed down again when the band played softer, or pantomimed the playing of various instruments, but on the whole the art of showmanship has become a shade more subtle. The bandmaster today is usually expected to be dignified, while at the same time maintaining a close and understanding relation with his audience.

The whole question of showmanship involves the bandmaster's choice of repertory as well as his personal appearance and mannerisms. The bandmaster must know what his audience expects to hear, and how it reacts to what he gives them. His problem is perhaps more many-sided than that of the symphony conductor or the dance orchestra leader, whose audiences expect a fairly established diet of Beethoven and Brahms from the one and popular tunes from the other. The bandmaster's programs must be varied to suit all sorts of tastes, and he must be prepared to keep step with his audience. It seems difficult, after listening to the radio with any regularity, to believe that anyone could ever underestimate the taste of an average audience, yet this is what bandmasters sometimes do. The bandmaster should be at least one jump ahead of his audience; the decline of the town band is at least in part due to the fact that audiences in so many cases have left their bandmasters far behind. There must be lots of light music on a band program; that everyone will admit. But, as I have argued elsewhere, there must today be some relief from a constant stream of the hackneyed and the trivial. Some bandmasters alienate not only serious listeners, but most of the rest of their audience as well, by the extreme vulgarity of some of their so-called "light" numbers. The people who would enjoy that type of light music do not, as a rule, attend band concerts; if they do, they are in a small minority. The band concert should include a variety of music, but excess of contrast defeats its purpose and displeases all types of listeners equally.

It is evidently desirable that the bandmaster be well schooled in general musical tradition, as well as in the particular traditions of band music. He must have an understanding and appreciation of the type of music that is the band's specialty and a sympathetic feeling for the type of musical duty the band is called upon to perform. But beyond this, if he is to perform concert music from the standard repertory, he must be familiar with orthodox "interpretations" of these works. One of the reasons that band concerts have enjoyed a certain disrepute among discriminating music lovers is that bandmasters have often programmed standard symphonic works (thereby lending tone to the program) and then conducted the works either in a wooden military manner or else with so superb a disrespect for the normal tempo, dynamics and phrasing that the listener wished the bandmaster had stayed with something he understood. Fortunately, the general level of musicianship among bandmasters is becoming higher, as recognition of the musical potentialities of the band becomes more widespread.

One of the questions invariably asked by persons listening to a band concerns the seating of the musicians. The conventional seating of the orchestra is more familiar: strings in front, grouped around the conductor, then the woodwinds, with the basses, brasses and percussion at the rear. Actually there is no set pattern of seating for either band or orchestra; placing the men so as to obtain the best blending of tone is one of the responsibilities of the conductor. Each conductor or bandmaster will have his own favored seating plan, some conforming in general outline to the more usual arrangements, others differing quite radically. It is often necessary to modify the seating arrangement because of the construction of the stage or platform, or because of special conditions encountered, for example, when playing out of doors. It was once customary among bandmasters to have the first clarinets immediately at their left

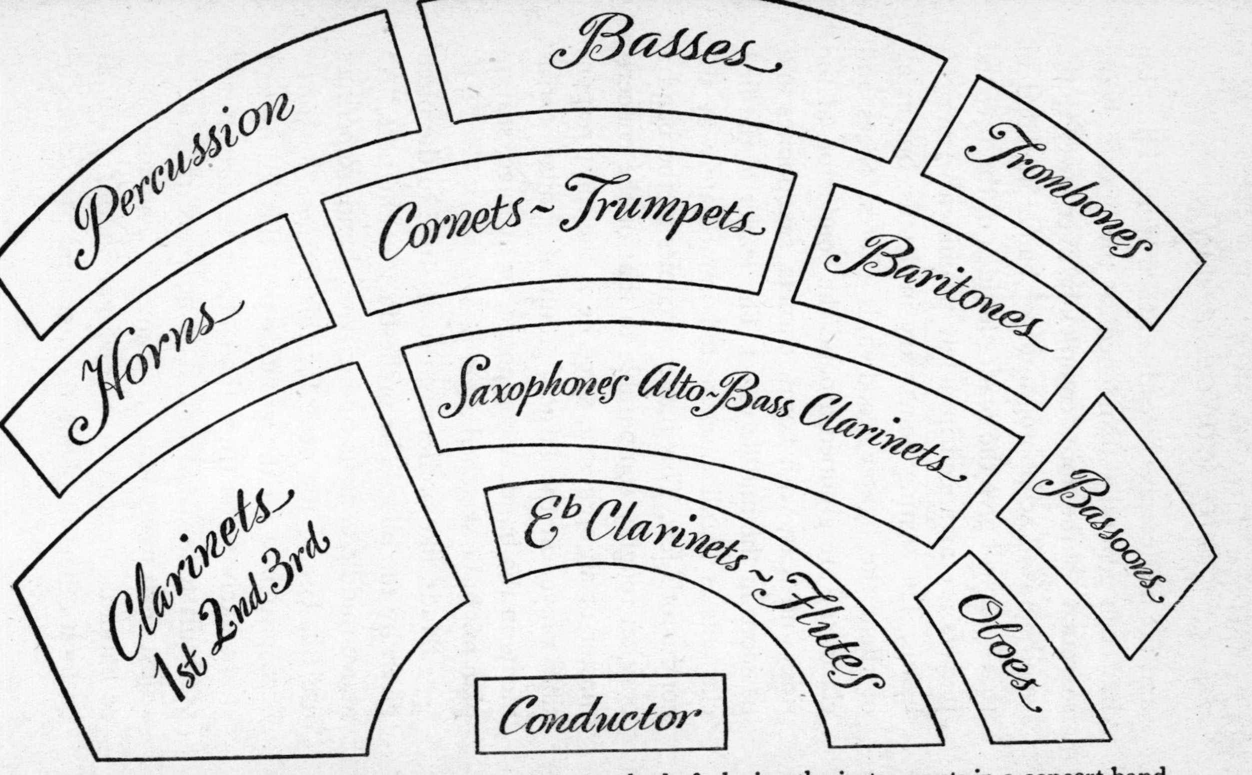

Diagram showing a fairly common, or average, method of placing the instruments in a concert band. Compare with photographs to note many variations of seating plan.

and the first cornets directly at their right. This plan has been generally abandoned, as the brasses, being so much to the fore, completely overpowered the woodwinds. The photographs of bands included in this book will give the reader an idea of the way the players are arranged in a few prominent American bands. The seating plans vary in details, but in all of them the lighter woodwinds (flutes, oboes and clarinets) are grouped around the conductor, at the sides and rear, with horns, cornets, saxophones and bassoons in the middle ranks. The leader of the first clarinets is in all cases seated immediately at the conductor's left. This player occupies in the band a position roughly comparable to that of the concert-master of an orchestra, since he is the most responsible player in the largest group of similar instruments in the band. A composite, or average, seating plan might be sketched as on p. 223.

Bands, like orchestras, usually tune to the pitch given by the oboe. The orchestra uses the note "A" above middle C as its tuning note; bands sometimes use B*b*. Use of the oboe for this purpose has often been criticized on the grounds that this instrument is not likely to be truer than others as instruments are built today, and that it is no more difficult to adjust than many other instruments. The conductor or bandmaster makes the decision on this point as on most others involving methods and procedures in his ensemble. Many bandmasters prefer to have the first clarinet player "sound his A," while others prefer to use a tuning bar or similar device.

The intonation of a band or orchestra is of course the responsibility of the conductor. He cannot himself tune each instrument, but he must be constantly on the alert to detect aberrations and call the attention of the players to them. Tuning an instrument before a performance does not mean that the instrument will of itself stay in tune. No wind instrument has ever been built with an absolutely perfect scale; the player must make constant adjustments to remain on pitch. Wind instruments are affected very greatly by heat and cold. Outdoor concerts are for that reason a special problem so far as intonation is concerned, as all instruments do not react to atmospheric conditions at the same rate or to the same degree. Heat tends to make the instruments sharper, while cold causes them to sound flat. Contrary to popular belief, moisture does not affect the intonation; it does, however, cause difficulty with the mechanisms of clarinets, flutes, saxophones and other instruments with keys.

The bandmaster and the band player must be prepared to cope with these difficulties, since so much band music is played in the open air. A well-constructed bandstand, preferably one of the shell type, is almost a necessity for open-air concerts. Such a

bandstand not only prevents the dissipation of sound, but shelters the players from sun and wind. I have heard band concerts played under a hot sun, with the band getting progressively sharper in pitch as the afternoon wore on. This was a matter beyond the control of the bandmaster or the players, who could only do their best and try to see that they all became *equally* sharp. Wind, heat and cold make outdoor concerts much more difficult for the players than the average listener ever realizes. But despite the difficulties and problems, the band is still the best instrument for outdoor music. Its tones blend and carry well, and it is less affected by atmospheric conditions than the orchestra, which in addition to having the same problems with the wind instruments, must cope with the deterioration of quality and resonance in the strings when the weather is humid.

The point has been made that with electrical amplification systems there is no reason why the orchestra cannot give outdoor concerts as effectively as the band. It is incontestable that amplification can make the orchestra as loud as the band; beyond that the argument does not have much weight. The advantage of the band lies precisely in the fact that amplification, with its inevitable distortion, is not necessary. A concert heard over an amplification system is no better, and in some respects not as good, as a concert heard over the radio. Furthermore, amplification does not of itself make the orchestra as adaptable or sturdy a combination as the band, or solve its more complex problem of intonation. It is true that there are series of outdoor summer concerts given by orchestras in many American cities and that in most cases amplification is not used. Such concerts, however, do not replace band concerts but supplement them. If there is a decline in the popularity of outdoor band concerts, it will not be because of competition from outdoor orchestra concerts; it will be because the standards of band performance and repertory fail to keep pace with the times. Outdoor concerts themselves will always remain a great popular attraction. No concert hall is large enough to accommodate all the people who want to hear live music, whether played by an orchestra or by a band; only the outdoor concert makes live music available to the countless thousands who seek to hear it.

One advantage the band retains with respect to outdoor concerts: tradition has it that the band concert is free. Even in the golden age in which we live, free concerts still have a meaning. There are not a few to whom even the modest admission usually charged at popular orchestra concerts means the difference between attending or not attending. Attendance at concerts of all sorts seems to prove that the radio is not yet a complete substitute for direct listening. The band, giving free open-air performances of a superior kind, fills a needed place in the musical life of the community, just as it does in providing the only live music in places where no orchestras can be established or maintained.

The concert band is heir to an honorable tradition of popular musicmaking, and though time has deprived it of some of its functions, it has acquired others and will adapt itself to further change. Despite many inconsistencies in its organization and practices, which we have noted, the band holds its immense following, and through its use as the principal musical organization in thousands of schools will attract still larger numbers of listeners in the future. Its character, and the character of its audience, may change, but we may safely assume that the main lines of its development are already indicated. The band has long since ceased to be primarily an appurtenance of the military; tradition will, no doubt, continue to demand that bands be maintained as part of the armed establishment, although it may be presumed that their military duties will become less and less what they were in the past. That bands should be maintained purely to provide for entertainment and relaxation is highly fitting; those functions more than justify the retention of bands in the armed services.

Whatever change future warfare or lack of warfare may bring to the military band, the concert band will hardly be affected. The concert band is firmly enough established as a civic and educational institution to survive the withering away of the martial associations of band music. Doubtless it will retain the military march as a staple of its repertory, as the great traditional musical form contributed by bands to music as a whole, even after marching on foot becomes as obsolete a part of war as fighting with bows and arrows. In a sense, the military march is already obsolete as a matter of military practice; the form is now another general musical form like the minuet or the waltz, capable of considerable elaboration.

It is true, I believe, that the future importance of bands as concert organizations depends on the cultivation of a special repertory, embracing the few traditional forms, such as the march, and the new special literature which alone can give musical meaning to band programs. To this I would add as much of the old "standard" repertory as the public still wants to hear, provided a surfeit is not already provided by orchestras and other ensembles, live or canned.

Bands are, of course, ideal organizations from the educational standpoint, and for the satisfaction of musical amateurs desiring to form and participate in instrumental ensembles. They serve in that way as the most practical vehicles for enabling large numbers of people to take an active part in making music. As concert organizations, bands at their best can be superb musical instruments. They can produce a variety of splendid sonorities, and can give fine performances of works which are well adapted to them. On a technical level, bands can play as precisely as good orchestras. They can, of course, be no better than their players, and certainly no band, even of the best players, can be better than its conductor. Bandmasters have the responsibility for the high or low regard in which bands and band music are held. The band is at its best when it is being most truly a band, when it is, in other words, operating on its own musical level and trying to be neither a symphony orchestra nor an overgrown novelty ensemble. The band is most entitled to serious consideration and respect when it is functioning as a natural expression of a flourishing popular musical culture.

Selected Bibliography

ADKINS, H. E.: *Treatise on the Military Band.* London: Boosey & Co., 1931.

BRENET, M. (M. BOBILLIER): *La Musique Militaire.* Paris: H. Laurens, 1917.

BRANCOUR, R.: "Musiques Militaires Belges," *Le Menestrel* (Paris), vol. 82, no. 36 (1920).

BUCHMAN, C.: "Composers Dedicate Works to the Band," *Modern Music* (New York), vol. XX, no. 1 (November, 1942).

CARSE, A.: *Musical Wind Instruments.* London: Macmillan, 1939.

CHIDESTER, L. W.: *International Wind-Band Instrumentation.* San Antonio: Southern Music Co., 1946.

CHIDESTER, L. W.: "Bands of Europe," *School Musician* (Chicago), vol. X (November-December, 1938).

CHIDESTER, L. W., and PRESCOTT, G. R.: *Getting Results With School Bands.* New York: Carl Fischer, 1938.

CHOP, M.: *Geschichte der Deutschen Militärmusik.* Hannover: L. Oertel, 1925.

CLAPPÉ, A. A.: *The Wind Band and Its Instruments.* New York: Henry Holt, 1911.

COMETTANT, O.: *Histoire d'un Inventeur au XIX Siècle* (Adolphe Sax). Paris: Pagnerre, 1860.

CORIBA, L.: "As Bandas Portuguesas e as Estrangeiras Comparadas," *Eco Musical* (Lisbon), vol. I, no. 47 (1911).

COURROYEZ, G.: *Etude sur les Musiques d'Harmonie.* Paris: Andrieu Frères, 1931.

DEGELE, L.: *Die Militärmusik.* Wolfenbüttel: Verlag für Musikalische Kultur und Wissenschaft, 1937.

DVORAK, R. F.: *The Band on Parade.* New York: Carl Fischer, 1937.

ELLIOTT, J. H., and RUSSELL, J. F.: *The Brass Band Movement.* London: J. M. Dent, 1936.

ESPINOSA, M. DE: *Toques de Guerra del Ejercito Español.* Burgos: 1939 (reprint of original, published at Madrid in 1769).

FARMER, H. G.: *Memoirs of the Royal Artillery Band* (An Account of the Rise of Military Music in England). London: Boosey & Co., 1904.

FARMER, H. G.: *The Rise and Development of Military Music.* London: W. Reeves, 1912.

FFOULKES, C.: *Notes on Early Military Bands.* London: Society for Army Historical Research, 1938 (vol. 17, pp. 188-200).

FIBULA, L.: "Per Una Partitura Unica di Banda," *Musica d'Oggi* (Milan), vol. 2, no. 11 (1920).

FRIES, J. H.: *Abhandlung vom Sogennanten Pfeiffer-Gericht.* Frankfurt, 1752.

GALLO, S.: *The Modern Band.* Boston: C. C. Birchard, 1935.

GODFREY, D.: *Memories and Music.* London: Hutchinson, 1924.

GOLDMAN, E. F.: *Band Betterment.* New York: Carl Fischer, 1934.

GOLDMAN, E. F.: *Amateur Band Guide and Aid to Leaders.* New York: Carl Fischer, 1916.

GOLDMAN, R. F.: *The Band's Music.* New York: Pitman Publishing Corp, 1938.

GOLDMAN, R. F.: "Bands in War-Time," *Modern Music* (New York), vol. XIX, no. 3 (March, 1942).

GRIFFITHS, S. C.: *The Military Band.* London: Rudall, Carte, 1896.

HAYES, G.: *King's Music.* London: Oxford, 1937.

HIBBERD, L.: "On 'Instrumental Style' in Early Melody," *Musical Quarterly* (New York), vol. XXXII, no 1 (1946).

HINDSLEY, M. H.: *Band . . . Attention!* Chicago: Gamble Hinged Music Co., 1932.

HOBY, C.: *Military Band Instrumentation.* London: Oxford, 1936.

HOBY, C.: "Wagner and Military Music," *Musical Progress and Mail* (London), October, 1933.

HUME, J. O., and ZEALLEY, A. E.: *Famous Bands of the British Empire*. London: J. P. Hull, 1926.

JOHNSTONE, A. E. (rev. by N. C. Page): *Instruments of the Modern Symphony Orchestra and Band*. New York: Carl Fischer, 1928.

KALKBRENNER, A.: *Die Organisation der Militärmusikchöre Aller Länder*. Hannover: L. Oertel, 1884.

KALKBRENNER, A.: *Wilhelm Wieprecht, Sein Leben und Wirken*. Berlin, 1882.

KAPPEY, J. A.: *Short History of Military Music*. London: Boosey & Co., 1894.

KASTNER, J. G.: *Manuel Général de Musique Militaire*. Paris, 1848.

LEIDZÉN, E. W. G.: *Invitation to Band Arranging*. New York: In preparation, 1946.

MAHAN, F. A.: "Military Band: History and Organization," *Journal of the Military Service Institution of the U. S.* (Governor's Island, N. Y.), 1908.

MILLER, G.: *The Military Band*. London: Novello, 1912.

NEUKOMM, E.: *Histoire de la Musique Militaire*. Paris: L. Baudouin, 1889.

PANOV, P.: *Militärmusik in Geschichte und Gegenwart*. Berlin: K. Siegismund, 1938.

PERRIN, A.: *Les Musiques Militaires.* Paris: Alcan-Lévy, 1882.

PORTEOUS, R.: *The Bandmaster's Atlas.* London: R. Cocks, 1854.

ROUSSEAU, J. J.: "Sur la Musique Militaire" (in *Ecrits sur la Musique*). Paris, 1838.

SCHEUNEMANN, G.: *Trompeterfanfaren, Sonaten und Feldstücke . . . des 16/17 Jahrhunderts.* Kassel: Baerenreiter Verlag, 1936.

School Music Competition-Festivals Manual. Chicago: Music Educators National Conference, 1943.

SOUSA, J. P.: *Marching Along.* Boston: Hale, Cushman and Flint, 1928.

THOMSON, V.: *The Musical Scene* (especially chapter on Transcriptions). New York: A. A. Knopf, 1945.

THOMSON, V.: "What Shall Band Music Be?" *Etude* (Philadelphia), July, 1942.

THOURET, G. (editor): *Musik am Preussischen Hof.* Leipzig: Breitkopf & Härtel, 1896.

U. S. WAR DEPARTMENT: AR 250-5 (Bands). Washington, October 24, 1945.

U. S. WAR DEPARTMENT: T/O & E 20-107 (Organization or Separate Band). Washington, March 8, 1944.

VESSELLA, A.: *La Banda dalle Origini Fino ai Nos-*

tri Giorni. Milan: Instituto Editoriale Nazionale, 1935.

WHITE, W. C.: *A History of Military Music in America.* New York: Exposition Press, 1944.

The reader will find many authoritative articles under various headings in standard musical dictionaries, such as Grove's *Dictionary of Music and Musicians, The Oxford Companion to Music,* etc., but will find few specific references to bands or their development in standard histories of music.

INDEX

INDEX